WHERE ARE YOU?

FINDING MYSELF IN MY GREATEST LOSS

M. J. FLOOD

En Route Books and Media, LLC
St. Louis, MO

ENROUTE
Make the time

En Route Books and Media, LLC
5705 Rhodes Avenue
St. Louis, MO 63109

Cover credit: TJ Burdick

Library of Congress Control Number:
2019949229

ISBN-13: 978-1-950108-38-1
ISBN-10: 1-950108-38-4

Dedication

To Tara, my love! My LOVE!!!!

Thank You and Acknowledgements

I have to start by thanking Alex Basile: you challenged me to write this. And it's been challenging. Thanks to Ken Frank for always being a great listener and reader. You're the first person who read this with a critical eye. Thanks to Gary Jansen for all of your encouragement and direction. Thanks to Ronda Chervin for reading and suggesting and ultimately putting me in touch with En Route Books and Media. And thank you Dr. Mahfood for considering *Where are You?* and for all of your guidance - and, of course, for publishing my story. And TJ Burdick at As You Wish, thanks for all your work making *Where Are You?* look like I wanted it to.

Thanks to the many, many people who read and offered support and praise.

Thank you to my family for letting me include our pain for "all to see." I think we've kept it private for long enough anyway.

Thank you to Charlotte and Judith for being my daily joy.

And to Tara, without you there'd be no story. Without you, there'd be no me.

And to Sophia...thank you, Little Birdy.

CONTENTS

Prologue

In 2016 someone who'd heard me speak of my experience of loss[1] at a memorial service suggested I "write a book." I smiled and said thank you as if I were receiving a compliment, but it is very possible that the woman who suggested I do so really meant "for me. You should write a book for me, for us—to read." I may have missed the point that writing of our troubles and our healing, or writing about anything, in fact, is an exchange between writer and reader, wherein we can all benefit. At the very least, writing—and reading—is a reminder that we are all here, together.

My pain of loss, after all that has been said and done, I think, has developed in me an awareness of the "other" in my life, which I had possibly been ignoring for various reasons.

I have wanted to write for as long as I can remember. Teachers, friends, and family throughout my life have encouraged me to write, but I always thought they were "putting me on," so to speak. As a child, I had envisioned scribbling away draft after painful draft, but I never really embraced the effort, though the effort was not what frightened me away. While I may have had many excuses—not having the right idea, not having the time, not wanting to disrupt my "status quo," not knowing how to submit a *manuscript*—I think now it has always been ego that has frightened me away

[1] See Appendix A

from my dream of writing. Afraid of being honest or vulnerable. Afraid of being rejected or—gasp!— *bad.*

Needless to say, I still have those fears, but I have been moved recently by a friend at work to write this all down. Alex Basile is a religion teacher, musician, and writer. He and I have been colleagues for two decades at Kellenberg Memorial, a Catholic high school in Uniondale, New York. Somewhat recently, I was troubled by some patterns I thought I might be developing in my thoughts and perspectives, so I mentioned my concerns to Alex. After some soul-searching direction, Alex asked if I'd ever written about my stories of loss. When I shared something with him, he suggested I "write a book."

This time I decided I should take that comment as a call to action, instead of a compliment.

I don't know what it was precisely, but a confluence of factors compelled me to sit down and start typing. In fact, this book began as a scribbling entry in a notebook, then a dictation into my phone, and then, finally, a daily routine of writing. Perhaps for the first time in my life, I demonstrated a bit of dedication to the writing process, writing a thousand or two words, a couple of hours a day, editing and revising.

But ultimately, and a conclusion I am only now starting to understand, it has been *loss* which has compelled me to write this book. The loss of my brother Brian. And even more greatly, the loss of my first child, my little baby Sophia. In truth, it is the sadness by which I feel I have been afflicted for the greater part of my memory that loss has proven to inoculate me of. This, now, *freedom* from the paralysis of disorientating depression has helped me to see the proverbial silver linings in even the greatest loss of my life and to *choose* joy.

One Sunday, just at that time that I began to mull over the idea for this endeavor, I was at Mass listening to the first reading about Adam and Eve in the garden just after their disobedient delight in the fruit of the Tree of Knowledge of Good and Evil.

In shame, Adam and Eve hid in the trees of the Garden when they heard God ask, "Where are you?"

Adam responded that he was afraid and ashamed—of his *nakedness*. He doesn't even admit to the apple! God *knows* the little man of clay that He'd made had eaten the apple *because* Adam hid himself in fear and shame!

I've heard and read this passage more times than I can really count, but I heard it again, and as if I'd heard it for the first time, I repeated to myself, "Where are you?"

It was one of those moments that "click" as though there were an *audible* click as so many thoughts came together like the wheel tabs of a combination lock.

It occurred to me, sitting in that pew, my three year old daughter thumping the top of my head like a bongo and my eight year old asking me if we can get donuts after Mass, that fear and shame—of the *self*—have forced me to hide behind my ego, my anger, my *loss*. I have hidden my "self" behind the death of my brother. I have *hidden* behind the death of my daughter. I have used her death to validate and *perpetuate* my "eyes closed" approach to life. All of this time, fear and shame have prevented me from looking at myself honestly, and loss has been hoisted like a golden god to lead a sad parade of idolaters like me.

That's what this book is about. Sort of.

So that day at Mass, that booming voice of God, snapped me to attention: "Where are you?"

And then I knew that I had some writing to do.

Where am I?

I've always had a sense of being lost.

I've always been, I think, disproportionately frustrated or irritated or angry and such whenever I've missed a turn or I've driven in an unfamiliar area, especially if I'd *expected* to be driving in a *familiar* area.

Even as a child, this was true. When I was seven, my family moved to Lynbrook on Long Island from Richmond Hill in the Borough of Queens, New York City. I remember, in those first days in my new suburban neighborhood, going for a walk with my mom and my aunt and my sister, who was just three or four years old and probably in a stroller. While now I remember precisely where I was when it happened, at the time, I experienced a moment of panic when, after racing ahead of my mother and unable to keep track of what direction I'd come from, I thought I was lost. My mother and aunt and sister came strolling by within seconds or tens of seconds anyway, but I can recall the disorientation I felt at the time, and I can place that disorientation throughout my life in various situations.

The sensation is a spinning of sorts, a quickening of time, and a cessation of cognition. Elevated pulse and sprinting breath—and other common symptoms of panic—are part of the mix, but that spinning sensation, I think, is most prominent. It's dreamlike sometimes, as in the dream when something malevolent lurks behind you and every time you spin, the "behind you" is now just behind you again, and spinning to see the thing simply becomes the reason you can't see the thing.

Since I was a teen—and a man after that—I have wondered pretty regularly where I would fit in or why I felt as though I didn't fit in anywhere. I wondered who liked me and who didn't. I wondered where I would end up. That familiar feeling of disorientation always accompanying those thoughts.

All I can really say at this point is that I have been lost for a long time. I don't know why.

Maybe that's the most frustrating part. Feeling a lifelong sense of disorientation, of being adrift, that seemed so close to sadness for so long and never really having a *reason* for that sense.

And then when something tragic came along, and I guess now enough of those things did come along, I could attach the sense to the tragedy and say, "Well there, that's why." When loss found me, in an odd way, I used it to put "life in order," so to speak. A sort of, "I knew that would happen" or "I expected that so I'm okay with it" rationale. But it's difficult to detect and debunk this *ex post facto* sort of logic when grief and pain are involved. It's difficult to see that what I think is "the way of things" is possibly the thing that leads me further astray. It's like looking at a map upside down—all the routes and signs and ways are there, but North and South are turned around.

I don't know. But I feel like I have a story to tell.

Where are You?

"Where are you?" I ask myself pretty regularly.

"Where are you?"

I guess it sounds more like the frustrated, upbraiding tone of a parent's spent patience, like Where are you *going*? or *What* are you *doing*?

But sometimes it's just a matter of fact location, as in I'm lost or something. Where am I? And sometimes it's an existential location, I guess. Like—in the "cosmos," or something. What world is this that I'm living in? What's my purpose? Things like that.

But I guess I also mean it for people—for others—people who maybe aren't here anymore. Wondering what has become of them. Places they've gone. Lives that have ended.

I'm lost though. I guess it's better sometimes to admit this. But in typical male fashion I'm the worst type of lost: I'm lost, but I act as if I know exactly where I am.

Tara

My wife Tara and I met the week of July 4, 1999 on the Jersey Shore's Long Beach Island. Some of "the guys" and I had been spending the week at my friend Jimi's shore house. Above the garage was a deck that we entertained on each night. On the last evening I was exhausted and decided to take a bit of a power nap before things really got "rolling." At some point my friend Mark shook me from bed and said to come on out.

Sleepily, I said, "I'll be out in a while."

Mark said, "No. Come on out now. You gotta see this girl."

So, I went out.

And there was this stunningly gorgeous girl-worth-a-thousand-ships girl. Her smile shook through the night, her eyes and nose said, "I am beautiful like time itself and mountains crumble at my sigh—and so will you." Her beauty was born on the coast of the Mediterranean three thousand years ago and it made the world stop and look and stop and look again. And I was defenseless, just as every smitten lover should be.

"Mike, this is Tara," Mark said.

I said hey and walked away with my beer and my diffidence, peeking over at her from time to time.

As the crowd diminished over the next hour or so, I joined the conversation of which she was part, but when she talked, the group disappeared, and when I talked, I was talking only to her.

I have a vivid recollection of being in my parents' Ford LTD station wagon when I was a child. I was in that "in between" stage of sleep and alert in the back seat leaning against my grandmother's shoulder and I could smell my mother's mother's coat, equal parts perfume and cigarette smoke—a smell I will never forget—and on the oldies radio station I heard The Flamingos' "I Only Have Eyes for You." When I met Tara in Long Beach Island, I knew that song again: "Maybe millions of people go by, But they all disappear from view, And I only have eyes for you." *Sha-bop, Sha-bop!* Boy, I was in *love*!

Tara was a no-nonsense business school student at Seton Hall in New Jersey. I was loafing around literature and philosophy classes at Queens College, working at a book bindery and "goin' out with the boys." She was Italian and I was Irish. She was four years my junior. I knew immediately we were opposites and I knew immediately that I was in love.

As the night rounded to an end, as she and her friend departed, I said goodbye.

And she said, "You're not going to ask me for my number?"

Shy little boy. We exchanged numbers.

For a while, I would tell friends that I was going to hang out with "that girl from Jersey." Then, after a while longer, they all knew "Tara." We were married on July 2, 2004. Of course, there's more to it all than that, but maybe some other time.

Tara and I gettin' married!

Sophia

In the spring of 2008 Tara and I conceived our first child. We were living in Long Beach, a barrier island on the Atlantic shore of Long Island, New York.

In Long Beach, you wear flip flops in the frozen-beach-February. Sweatpants and Uggs are requisite wardrobe. In Long Beach—all things are "cool." Living there, in our sixth floor apartment with a Manhattan-view balcony (as the realtor advertised), meant Tara and I (and all of the twenty-something residents that called Long Beach home) were committing to a life of peace and "chill" times, laid back dinners, care-free walks to the beach, and so on and so on.

Life was good. Everything was going according to plan. Everything on schedule. Tara and I felt so "in control." We did what we wanted. We were accomplishing what we hoped. What we planned for materialized.

Tara's belly was growing. We were planning. Proud grandparents were glowing. Friends were high-fiving. We're keeping the gender secret—it's a girl. I had hoped so. We will name her Sophia Michelle.

We are buying you clothes now. And books now, Sophia. We are calling you Little Birdy now. I am singing to Mama's belly now. I am talking to Mama's belly. I am singing to you, little baby. I am talking to you, Sophia. I am your daddy, little girl.

Autumn in Long Beach. Thanksgiving. Christmas is

coming and we're expecting our first child in the late winter.

Hurt

Tara is a worrier. She is worried.

"Everything is going to be OK," I say.

"I don't feel the baby moving."

"It's OK. The baby's getting bigger now. There's not enough room for her to move around like that anymore."

"Something's wrong."

"Everything's OK. Don't worry."

That was December 3, 2008. Evening. We went to sleep. We went to work.

My cell phone vibrates in my pocket regularly while I'm at work. Normally I leave the vibrating nuisance in my pocket and check missed calls at some point later on. But that morning, for some reason, I pulled my cell from my pocket and saw that Tara was calling. This was very uncommon, so with a suspicion of dread I answered in the middle of class.

She said, "The baby's not moving. The doctor told me to go to the hospital."

I left class immediately. I sped over to Tara's office. She got in. I held her hand. She was crying.

"Everything's gonna be OK," I say.

Is it a lie when we speak with certainty about something we don't actually know with certainty? I know as we drove to the hospital I believed —it might be OK. It doesn't have to be the worst. We are so blessed. Everything is going according to plan. Why should it be the worst? There's no reason to believe that. I said some Hail Marys just in case.

"Everything's going to be OK," I said as I drove to the hospital in my dark thoughts of the worst.

At the hospital a nurse told us, "I'm sorry. I don't hear a heartbeat. The baby's gone."

Tara cried out. I've always thought of it as a howl. I've never heard that sound from her, before or since. I can hear it still in my mind—the forever and repeating echo of death.

I shared a few choice words with the doctor and nurses on hand. Of course, that's foolish. I suspect they understood. But Sophia was gone.

Gone? Where to? Where is she? I don't understand.

"How do we get the baby out?" I asked.

"Delivery."

Tara groaned then cried.

"Do you want to have an autopsy?" The nurse asked me.

"No."

"Do you want the baby to be buried?"

"What happens if we don't?" I asked.

The nurse averted her eyes, and responded, "Discarded—with medical waste."

I am in a dream. Could you imagine? The child in the womb of her mother, to be thrown out with the trash? Could you imagine a grown child, or a parent, now deceased, to be thrown out with the trash?

"No. We'll have a funeral," I said.

Sophia's grandparents come in. I'm not sure they understand. Maybe they do. They look as concerned as they'd be if Tara were going in for a surgery. My mother is talking about whatever—this is a defense mechanism for her, I guess. I ask her to stop. I hope she's not hurt. My mother-in-law says she's lost faith in everything. I doubt that. I'm sure she doesn't know what else to say. My father-in-law can't even sit in the room. He's outside by himself in the hallway.

If it were their eight or ten or twenty-year-old grandchild, they'd be sobbing. Wrenching of clothes and hair. Lamentations. I don't think they really understand. Maybe I'm angry at them for not understanding. Maybe they are just trying to be strong. Maybe I am the one who doesn't understand. Maybe I shouldn't be so bitter, but I'm angry. No. I'm not angry. I'm angry when someone cuts me off on the road. I'm angry when I don't get Wi-Fi. I'm not angry right now. I'm enraged. I'm devastated. I'm heart broken. I'm trapped. I want to bite. I want to kill. I want to tear it all down. I want to do unto others what the world has done unto me.

My dad puts his hand on Tara's leg, covered by the blanket of a hospital bed. He says, "I wish I could take this pain for you." I believe him. He would if he could. Perhaps he already has.

Labor is induced. A dose of pitocin administered by some doctor: vague, nameless, distant—uncaring, I fear.

We stay overnight. Hours of labor. I tell Tara she's doing great. I almost forget that Sophia isn't really coming to us. I feel like a proud father.

Then I remember. I think: I've never felt so sad and alone.

The baby is coming. I can see her head. I think I love her.

Then I think there is no life there.

She is tiny.

The nurse took her lifeless body aside to clean her and dress her.

"She's beautiful," the nurse said. And with just the faintest singsong joy, she said, "I think she looks like *daddy*."

I felt that joy shamefully for a nanosecond before I felt the reproachful touch of prideful anger: "Don't talk to me of her beauty!" I thought. "Don't tell me she *looks* like me! She's dead!"

It would take me *years* to realize what a kindness that nurse provided me.

The nurse returned to place my baby in a bassinet. My baby wore a knit hat. She was wrapped in a sweater, a guardian angel pinned to the sleeve.

The nurse asked if we would like to hold her. I said yes. I pressed my lips to her face. Tara unwrapped the sweater from Sophia and took the cap from her head. We looked at her body. My little girl. Cold and still and gone.

“Where Are You, Sophia?”

I was mowing my lawn one day and a little bird fluttered and perched on a fence only a few feet away. I stopped pushing the mower and stood there looking at it. Then I killed the motor. The bird stayed perched on the fence post. Silly as this may sound, it was looking at me. Staring, really. So, I stepped towards it. When it didn’t move, I imagined the bird hopping from its fencepost to perch upon my extended index finger like a picture of St. Francis I’d seen somewhere. That would have been magical. But it didn’t move, and I didn’t take another step. It was only a few feet away from me. I figured it would have flitted away by then. I was surprised, but I didn’t want it to flit away so I didn’t take another step because then it wouldn’t be so remarkably different. It wouldn’t have been special. If I had closed the distance further, the bird would have darted off and I would have been disappointed by the ordinariness of the encounter. So, I took a step away and then another. And I turned my back. When I turned again to pull the lawn mower ripcord, the bird was gone.

I said, “Where are you?”

I spoke aloud like a fool and suddenly lost my breath and grew teary-eyed.

I knew who that Little Birdy was. I knew that that bird perched there for me to see and to think of Sophia.

Some Joy for Your Suffering, and Some Suffering for Your Joy

I'm 42 years old now. I was 32 when we lost Sophia. This December will be 10 years since she died, since she was born, since we saw her for the first-and-never-again-time. Ten years and I remember it like it was yesterday. Not the details, but the feeling. I *feel* it like it was yesterday. The pain. But some of the secret pleasures or joys, too. There were some. I say secret because it's hard to admit or explain how any joy can come from this devastation or exist in the time of the devastation. But come they do. Come they must. Sometimes the bereaved, myself included, reject those joys. I think we feel unworthy of joy while we grieve. I think our feelings of guilt wish for us to suffer for, to pay for, the loss we were part of, for the loss we most *certainly* caused. No smiling. No laughter. No joy. Pain only please. Suffer hard.

The night of December 4, Tara's contractions were being monitored. The hospital room was dark and quiet. She was resting. I was sitting in the chair beside her. I was watching TV without the volume. Seinfeld was on. I was laughing to myself.

I smelled the faintest whisper of smoke. Yet not quite smoke. No. Burning rubber. Hmph.

When the scent grew in intensity, I became more alert. Its origin was nearby. I sat up. Something was burning in there.

"What's the matter?"

"You smell that? Something's burning."

Then there was smoke. From the radiator in the room. I rang the nurse's station.

"Oh! Oh no!" chirped a nurse, who, while I'm certain in the case of medical emergency or irregularity would be cool as a cucumber, in this case of a *mechanical* emergency, was suddenly inarticulate and panicky. She ran out of the room! Uhhh...I looked for a fire extinguisher.

The nurse and more returned. Tara was carted out of the room in a hurry and I followed her to another room.

I reentered to retrieve some of our belongings. The radiator was aflame. An electrician was tending to the heater while what looked like a janitor stood to his side with the fire extinguisher.

When I got back to the new room, Tara was situated, and my eyes were wide with a kind of "wtf" wonder.

"Is this for *real*?"

"The fucking thing's on fire, Tara!"

We laughed. Ain't *that* somethin'? We laughed. We were awaiting the birth of our first and beloved and lifeless child, but there was a laugh. As if things weren't bad enough, our room goes on fire!? We laughed. Laughter is the weed in the garden of pain, that's for sure.

Later that night, in our new room, I grew exceedingly uncomfortable in the chair beside Tara's bed. A nurse, sensing my discomfort, indicated that the chair folds out to a single bed. Oh, sweet heaven! The nurse brought sheets, a pillow, and a blanket. I snuggled with great comfort and laughed. Tara, knowing how happy a comfy spot makes me, laughed too.

But in the morning of December 6, we were reminded of

where we were and why we were there. Suffering is king and we were the welcomed guests of his castle.

I was hungry. Tara said she didn't feel like eating. She didn't want to leave her room. I went outside where there was a little breakfast bar. Cereals. Bagels. Juices. Fruits. Women, smiling, walking around in robes and slippers. I was the only man. They were all mothers. I brought back some bagels and didn't tell my wife about what I saw. As we ate our bagels, we heard a woman cry out in pain. We stopped mid chew – then we heard the cry of the newborn baby.

A room away from us in that hospital, the greatest of all joys, of which we were just denied, greeted a new mother.

"I am suffering. I am pain. I will show *you*! This is what you get for your laughter and your little joys and comforts."

And this is the impression with which we entered our new lives without Sophia. Everyone else's joy is our pain. That's the genesis of the infant loss grief. It's difficult to see any joy in this world. Other people's weddings, job promotions, birthdays all have the smoke of ruin over them for the bereaved. Holidays are cursed. Even other people's baby announcements are bitter reminders of loss. It's difficult to transcend the self-oriented position of loss.

Leaving without Our Baby

When we were discharged from the hospital, we slinked away in shame. Leaving without our baby. My God. It still seems too awful to actually have happened. Judith, Tara and my second baby girl after Sophia, was born at 32 weeks. She was in the NICU for ten days. We left the hospital without her too. And having the horror of Sophia's death in our minds, leaving Judith was especially painful, but leaving without Sophia was—well, I'm not sure, I'm not a psychologist, but it didn't seem real. As it happened, I doubted it was happening. I think that's trauma.

Eyes cast down, we left the hospital. Maybe we held hands. Maybe I walked ahead of Tara to block, so to speak. I don't remember. I remember bits of it like a dream. My subconscious was working overtime as we exited. This is not real.

"This is not real. You can blink and be in another place if you just believe it hard enough. This is not real. Eat something. Drink something. Turn on a TV. Do something. You'll see this is not real," my deep, deep id says to protect me from the too horrible to believe, the bone crushing, castrating horror of reality, the eviscerating "real."

Our parents were there then like a security team flanking us, a phalanx of broken hearts around the empress and emperor of despair. Their aimlessness of worry and doubt and confusion in the maternity ward only a day or so ago was now replaced with the task-oriented decisiveness of an exit strategy, whose goal was to protect Tara from any additional hurt. We had a planned departure from the hospital and reentry to the apartment in Long Beach. Who was designated to get Tara's car from her work in Garden City, left there from the day before last? Who was designated to get to the apartment ahead of us and call the elevator so that we wouldn't have to wait in the lobby? Who was to unlock the apartment door for us? There was a plan, but I don't remember. It's a blur.

When Tara and I exited the hospital, the parking attendant, some kid, took my ticket. He must have read the code on the ticket, because he said, "Congratulations, man."

I think I put my hand up as if to say stop right there. I told him, "We lost the baby. Please. Don't say ANYTHING to my wife."

Leaving the hospital without my baby. That was an emptiness that I found difficult to explain. Or fill.

Condolences

I read many condolences and listened to many as well. But every time someone spoke or every time we opened a "sympathies" note, my heart stopped, and I wanted to cover Tara's ears. So often others' words are gentle and kind and loving, but so many people possessed such different understandings of what "healing" is and what "grief" is.

I wanted to protect Tara. I wanted to protect myself. But from what? From others' sympathy? From others' care? No. I guess that's not it. From others' insensitivity? Sure. There's a lot of that without a doubt. People say all kinds of things.

People told me and Tara to get back to work—as if our careers had a healing power that would somehow assuage the pulverized hearts our zombie-bodies shuffled around. People told me to just get Tara pregnant again. You know—like a new goldfish in the bowl. People told us not to wait too long to try again. You know—her clock is ticking and what not. Really numbskull type stuff. There's also the fear for a mother that people might view her as "incompetent" in some way, incapable of "being a mother." Like impotence for a man, there is a gender expectation. It's sad and wrong, as most expectations are, but it's real, and Tara and I were afraid of it.

Perhaps the trickiest thing to navigate is the question of value. Philosophical arguments abound regarding the nature and value of life—particularly "unborn" life—but also critical life, disabled life, end of life, terminal life, vegetative life and so on, but it's useless for me to explore those here because to Tara and me, Sophia had value. Even if that value was limited to potential—she had value. So, I am aware of a potential conflict between our assessment of Sophia's value and others'. And that can be hurtful. I know Sophia had a heartbeat. I heard it. I know what she looked like. I have photos. I know I prepared for her to be here. I know I buried her. I know I went to visit her at the Cemetery every week. How would something without value command such action? Or maybe I was just crazy. Needless to say, I felt that I might be. Or that people thought I might be. All because I loved a baby that never "was."

Nobody thinks you're crazy—or no one, at least, would blame you—for grieving the passing of your parent. Or a sibling. An old friend. An aunt, uncle or grandparent. Not even grieving a pet is so unbelievable. An infant or child might be one of the most grievous of all losses. But a stillborn. Somehow, that's different. To some, anyway. Or to most, maybe.

I'm not going to pretend like I always know the right thing to say. And I'm certainly not writing to put anyone on blast. I think there is a dearth of knowledge about communicating with the bereaved. That's a different story for someone far better informed than I, though.

A Little Box for Sophia

By December of 2008, by the time Sophia was taken from me, Tara and I had collected some small amount of baby clothes for Sophia. Some books and toys. Baby stuff. Bottles and bibs. We donated most of them to St. Mary of the Isle in Long Beach. I remember the priest who came to our apartment asked if we would want to keep anything for when we conceived again. (It's important to me that I mention that he *did* say "when". It was, to him, a certainty. How little did he, and so many others, know how distant that certainty was to us. The death of a baby, a "fetal demise" as some call it in our case, makes family making a dream beyond the grasp. We of course, could not say "when". We could only say "if" we conceived again. And even *if* we conceived, we knew taking our pregnancy to term was not a foregone conclusion). It was thoughtful of him, but "hand me downs" from a stillborn wasn't what I had in mind.

We kept some of the things. Special little bits of clothing. We keep them in a box. It's made of wood. Cedar maybe. I only think so because it smells so nice. A bird is painted on its hinged lid. It's now on our bedroom dresser. It has a few keepsakes of Sophia's: the sweater and cap she was first dressed in, a picture of her from the hospital, some thoughtful sympathies from loved ones, friends and family and acquaintances. Tara and I open it from time to time. It's always emotional. I smell the sweater and cap when I open the box. I think it smells like Sophia, but it just smells like the box. But I think it smells like her. It's a sad thought to think she *is* that box now.

Where are You?

"Where are you, Sophia? Are you there in that box? Are you in the ground beneath your grave marker? Sometimes I want to lie down on the earth at the door of your grave and dig my arms down and cradle the shoebox sized coffin we buried you in and bring you up, earth and box and all, and pull you to my heart and hug you, earth and box and all, and cry for you, earth and box and all."

I don't understand why we don't all dive into the graves of our loved ones and embrace their bones and hug them. It seems reasonable enough to me to do so. I can't accept the barrier between life and death. I can't understand living when death is now. Sophia, I want to follow your infant soul to the unknowable and hold you all along the way forever.

You were only two and a half pounds. You were so close to nothing but so far from it. And *now* you're so close to nothing and so far from it. *Nothing* can be more disorienting than the death of a child in the womb.

At Holy Innocents where all the children are buried in St. Charles Cemetery, Sophia's grandparents and my siblings gathered for a small service. There was so little to say. But I told everyone, "What your children, my nephews and nieces, mean to me, I hope my daughter can mean to you. I wanted her so badly. Her name is Sophia Michelle." And that was pretty much it. Tara and I sat with the little box for a few minutes. I wanted to pick it up. Are you really in there? Can I hold you? Can I press you close to my heart and keep you there forever? How long can I stay here with you? Can I die and as if from a jet in the sky dive into nothingness until I overtake you and from the nothingness grab you? I wanted you so bad. Where are you?

Strangers in Healing

When that nurse told us my baby Sophia was gone—I don't know how Tara...It is still difficult to understand and equally difficult to talk about. I guess that's still part of the healing dilemma. I have tried to think what it must have felt like—in fact, Tara has told me—to have a lifeless child inside you. This is all I can imagine: think of your child. Your son or daughter. Where is he now? Is she at school? Is he married? Maybe you have grandchildren. I want you to think right now—the phone is ringing. Answer it. The voice on the other end is telling you that your child is dead. Your grandchild is dead.

How do you feel? Well you're getting there. But the truth is that you can't really imagine it.

And I feel the same way about my wife. I can't understand what she experienced—and continues to experience. Sophia was everything we hoped for and dreamed of and she was our daughter, even if she weren't yet born. And then Tara learned that Sophia, still in Mama's belly, was no longer alive. In her womb! In that place so ostensibly sacred and safe.

It seemed to me that I hoped for shared experience of pain and recovery between me and Tara. And at first, that's the case. Our loss seemed to be an "us against the world" affair until we had our first disagreement about whatever nonsense like dinner or front- or back-facing toilet paper. Maybe it was something more substantial about intimacy or communication or maybe something insensitive was said about feelings or loss or healing. But before long our partners can at times seem like part of the world we were just recently combatting together. Before long, our partners, in the tragedy of a loss like ours, can seem so distant that we're not sure things could ever be the same again.

There are some chasms of experience that can't be bridged. Or not without abundant difficulty, the kind of difficulty that challenges everything about our notions of "being". Or maybe it's just that those bridges are so difficult to form that keeping the distance might seem easier. In other words, it seems easier to *avoid* understanding and accepting each other's unique experience and relationship to loss, each other's healing pace. Sometimes it just seems easier to believe that the "us against them" approach will prevail by providing a common cause. In the long run, of course, that's untrue, that commonality of cause is contrived—it's a defense mechanism, not too unlike mob mentality. But such "long vision" is difficult at times like those.

I wanted to understand, but I was afraid I wouldn't ever. Or perhaps, I was simply afraid that to understand meant the pain would simply start anew or double its effect.

How Do You Feel?

My reluctance to be completely honest with anyone is something I should really have explored.

A guy I worked with, his name was Tim, asked me how I was feeling when I got back to work. It was probably about a week after we lost the baby. I don't think Tara went back until the new year. I probably shouldn't have either.

But Tim came up to me, we had lunch supervision together, and he shook my hand and said, "I wanted to give you a hug, but I don't want to crowd you. So I'll just shake your hand. How are you doing? How're you feeling?" He was smiling warmly and, with a genuine sense of concern, looking in my eyes. As I said, he was about the nicest guy in the world, and I felt the need or comfort to be honest with him so I didn't want to dismissively tell him it was all gonna be ok and Tara and I are strong and we'll get pregnant again and have a family and blah blah blah blah lies and so on.

So, I shook his hand and leaned into him and said deliberately with intermittent pauses, "I want to shoot myself in the face."

When I released his hand and stepped away from him, he shook his head and looked at me. His eye gave birth to a tear he wiped quickly away with the hand I'd just released from the embrace he'd offered.

"I'm sorry," I said. "That was too much. That's not what you wanted to hear, is it?"

"I wanted to hear," he said, looking in my eyes again in that same sincere way, "*whatever* you wanted to say. I can't imagine what you're feeling. I'm sorry you have to go through this."

That was about the most honest thing I may have said to anyone—at least at that early stage—about Sophia. And his response was about the most perfect thing anyone said to me.

And I might have been *snapping* at him. What a dick, right? Like I was already sick of the platitudes and I was gonna let it rip, you know, because I was probably bitter, and I certainly didn't understand why I was off charading at work when Tara was still at home—alone. Christ. I *felt* alone when I was surrounded by people and busy at work and she was at home, *actually* alone. With nothing to do but think.

Thinking. Jesus, help the bereaved with their thinking, please. It is the *worst* thing to do while healing, but the *only* thing to do to heal. Like the pain of setting a broken bone or the burn of disinfecting an open wound. But thinking, especially thinking *alone,* when you're grieving is hellish. Reliving the event in every awful detail. Everything to be seen and heard and smelled again. And not to mention reliving the events that preceded the tragedy. Considering every little fragmented memory of a decision or an action that could have been made in some alternative way and so have changed the direction of the earth's revolution and made every bad thing that happened NOT happen. Thinking is the petri dish for every guilt created, every shame felt, every slight (imagined or real) delivered. And from that same dish comes every spontaneously generated saving grace. Every hope realized. Oh, it's a mess at times, for sure.

Anyway, Tim was a good guy. I don't remember Tim's last name. Like I said, he was about the nicest guy in the world. From what I remember, he was a Wall Street guy who said he'd had enough of the sliminess and wanted a job that would be more rewarding or fulfilling. He only worked at my school a year. I don't know why he left. And I don't know where he went afterwards.

Someone else asked me how I felt, I don't remember who it was, but I just said, "Scotch. Cigarette. Handgun." That was pretty mean. I don't even *own* a handgun. But I was making a point. It was crassly made but it was the point all the same. I felt terrible. I was profoundly sad and disoriented.

Another person came up to me and shared that he and his wife had had several miscarriages but that things worked out and they had beautiful children after all.

I looked dumbly at him and said, "It's different. It wasn't a miscarriage. I held her. I held my dead baby."

He teared up and I'm not sure why—I didn't ask and I never talked to him about it, but maybe he teared up because the idea that I held Sophia's lifeless body moved him, or maybe he teared up because I was so dismissive of his own experience with his loss.

When I think about it now, I realize that an infant loss is an infant loss. I shouldn't have said that to him. I know that every loss is different, of course, but I don't think that's what I meant when I told him that. I meant that my loss was *worse*.

But I didn't want to be told that things would improve. I wanted to hear that my pain was real, and it was okay to sit in it for a while or forever for that matter. One co-worker came up to me and told me that he and his wife suffered an infant loss and that they still go to the cemetery, that they used to go every week but now it's not so frequent, but they still go. That made me feel better—that he was still mourning his loss and remembering his forever baby. I *did* want to hear that other people had infant losses like mine, miscarriages, stillbirths, SIDS, and so on because I didn't want to feel alone, but I didn't want to hear—yet—that everything was going to be okay for my nice little family and our first baby girl in her cold grave.

Losing Things I

When I received my first communion, I was seven years old, in Saint Raymond's in East Rockaway. My parents bought me a watch. It was digital. In the daytime a little digital sun appeared on the face and in the evening, a moon. It had a light to read the time in the dark. I loved it.

At some point after, I tried to take the watch off, but the clasp was stuck. I was only seven years old. I became instantly frustrated. I growled and pulled fiercely at the wristband, which, unable to endure the strain, broke, sending the watch-face across the room, against the wall and to the floor. When I picked it up, the watch-face was blank. The light didn't work. The sun and the moon didn't appear. I threw it in the trashcan and cried. I put crumples of paper on top of it in the trashcan. I never told my parents.

Losing Things II

When I was a little kid, I had a purple Mako Shark Corvette Matchbox car. It was the envy of the boys on the block. It rolled better than any other Matchbox car. And it was rare. *No one* ever saw one like it.

I loved that car. I used to have a Hot Wheels Dragway racetrack. You'd place the car in one of two tracks and roll it back against a spring-loaded launch space. Another car could be placed beside it and then a release button simultaneously sent the cars flying down a track a few yards long. We'd race cars like that for hours.

Sometimes we'd place bets on the races and wager our different cars. We all had favorites. And the Mako was mine. It *never* lost. My pals would only race me on condition that I not use the Mako. They all wanted it. I don't know how many baseball cards or comic books or GI Joes were offered for that car. I always said no. That car was awesome.

But then it was gone. My parents had company, and it was gone. There were kids there, but I can't believe someone would've stolen it. I mean the car was cool, but the kids that were at the party weren't the neighborhood boys that knew of the legend of the Mako Shark. Did I boast of the Mako to these kids? Did I simply fawn? Was the wonder of this little car innately alluring? I don't know, but it was gone. I looked *everywhere*. Everywhere.

Trust me. I'm a good "looker". When I lose something, I can really look for it. Obsessive, really. I cried and told my parents someone stole it. I accused their *friends'* kids. My parents are good people and wouldn't believe someone stole something. Or maybe they just didn't want to ask their friends to interrogate their kids. Or maybe they thought I lost it (clearly, they didn't know how much I loved that car). Or maybe they didn't care that I lost a stupid car.

But I looked in every corner of my house. It was gone. And I looked for a *long* time. The truth is, I still look! And I don't know how funny this is (I should really tell my therapist about this), but if I go to my folks' to find a tool in my dad's cellar or to look for some old albums or photos, I'll move some random boxes around just to see if I can find it.

I think about the feeling of finding that thing. I'd be overjoyed. I might cry.

Losing Things III

My daughter Charlotte saw a balloon floating away in the sky one day. She was about two or so. It wasn't her balloon. It was some helium balloon floating maybe a block or two away up up up and she started to sob.

She was really crying, and she said, "It's Sarah's balloon!"

I was confused, so I questioned her gently.

She thought it was my niece's balloon. We'd given Sarah a balloon for her birthday. It was *months* ago. It was NOT Sarah's balloon. But to Charlotte, that balloon that she gave her "big" cousin was the *only* balloon in the world. And her child's mind couldn't understand the gravity of the loss. I tried to explain that it wasn't Sarah's balloon.

"Sarah's balloon is at her house," I tried to explain—realizing that that was a lie and all that faulty explanation would do was make Charlotte believe that the next time we went to Sarah's house, she could expect to see the balloon. Apparently, I couldn't muster the strength or logic to explain that things don't last forever.

"It's someone else's balloon," I said in an attempt to change directions, hoping that would diminish her sense of loss.

Charlotte said, "Whose?"

I said I didn't know. Some person. Some other person lost a balloon. She said that's sad too Daddy. And she cried some more.

So, I hugged her and said I know baby. Because she was right. It *was* sad.

Loss Stew

There are many ingredients to loss stew. It is a hearty dish. It serves everyone a filling meal at one time or another. Some get to eat from their bowl many times. Some take a bit here and there. Some eat straight from the pot in which it's made. These are its ingredients. Add to taste:

I am the only person in the world
I can't sleep
I am tired
I can't breathe
I am nervous
I don't care anymore
My heart is racing
I feel pressure in my chest
I feel a thrushing in my arm
I'm having a panic attack
I'm having a heart attack
I am afraid
I hear water rushing through my ear
I can't concentrate
I'm snapping at everyone
I don't deserve love
I deserve more
I want to drink
I want to die

I feel claustrophobic everywhere
I'm smoking again
I want to break something
I want to be *ill* so I don't have to *pretend* to be *ok*
I think I have cancer
Something is coming to get me
I'm not hungry
All I want to do is eat
I'm losing weight
I'm gaining wait
I need to be saved
I need to be left alone
I don't want to get out of bed
I can't get out of bed
I won't get out of bed
I'm going to rip the fucking *phone* out of the wall!
I have road rage
Let's get fucked up
All I want is you!
Stay away from me!
I want to go away
I want to move
I never want to leave the house again
I'm going to feel this way forever
I need a new job
I don't want to work again
Let's get a dog
Let's have another baby
We'll never have a baby
I don't want to have a baby
Where are my friends?
Who are my friends?
I have no friends
I. AM. SO. ALONE.

Float Away

Sometimes I wish I could stand on top of something tall and towering, something from which to look out over the world, the globe, the heavens and breathe through my mouth and let the wind knock the breath from my lungs and spread my arms wide and fly away like a kite loosed from its cord.

Where are They?

Where are you, Sophia, my sweet little baby?
Where are you, Brian, my poor lost brother?
Where are you Jeanne Marie?
Where are you Frank and Doug?
Where are you Tommy?

Where are these people I know who died so suddenly? So young? Where do they go? Some of them I only knew for a short time, so why don't I forget them? Some of them I hardly knew. Would I forget them if I had the choice? If they didn't *die*, would I remember them? Would I be better off if I could erase the devastation? Why does losing them make me feel so lost?

Frank was a boy in my homeroom. In tenth grade he took his own life. I think that might have been the first person that I knew, independently, that died. And certainly, the first person I knew who committed suicide. I don't remember, and it's not my story to tell, but I was at the funeral and I remember his sister processing out of the church and she was wearing his clothes. I think his jacket and tie and an overcoat of his, if I remember correctly. Little did I know how well I would come to know her pain one day, but at the time I only saw a little girl in her brother's clothes, and I thought that she must feel so sad.

Doug died in a fight. He was struck with a bat or a club or a stick during an altercation. He apparently seemed well enough immediately afterwards so his friends took him home.

He died in his sleep. He was a good guy. Funny as hell. I played lacrosse with him for a little while in high school. I think I must have been nineteen or so when he died. So, we had graduated high school already. A former classmate called me and asked if I'd heard about Doug. He told me what happened, and we went to the funeral together.

I remember seeing some old high school friends at the funeral mass and one of them saying "if it weren't for weddings and funerals". We were kids for crying out loud and already trading empty platitudes about death. We were kids at a *kid's* funeral, so who could blame us for not knowing any better than to repeat the emptiness we'd heard baffled adults utter to each other?

But I guess that's death. We are all clueless.

Tommy died. That one hurt. Of course, now I know they all hurt, but he was a good buddy. Again, these aren't my stories to tell, but I feel like I have to. Tommy was so good. Our friendship started out when we recognized we liked the same music. Then we hung out once or twice. He was smart and funny and generous.

We were walking back to my house one night. We were seniors in high school. We were cutting through a school yard. My brother Brian had died some months before.

Tommy asked, "Wanna sit and talk for a while?"

I said sure, so we sat on a schoolyard bench.

I figured we'd talk about nonsense, but he said, "Can you tell me about your brother?"

What a brave kid. We talked about my brother Brian, his illness and death. I'll never forget that.

Tommy died. By then we'd drifted apart, but it was very very very sad. Again. Just a kid.

Just a kid. All kids. And I haven't ever really processed what it all meant to me. And I haven't even begun to talk about Jeanne Marie.

Jeanne died driving from Long Island to a friend's place in Pennsylvania to kick off the summer the morning after her senior prom. She was driving a small group of friends. She fell asleep at the wheel and was thrown from the car.

We were all graduating. We were seniors and pumped for what we'd hoped might be a great summer. I'd known Jeanne since I was in second grade. Jeanne and the girls were like sisters. We'd all known each other since grade school. We were all crushed. She might have been the friendliest, happiest girl I knew.

I came home from a show—Beastie Boys, I think—and when I came home from the train, my mother and sisters were in the front room of my house. Of course, I knew, as one does in such scenarios, that something was wrong.

My sister said, "Something bad happened."

My mother, interjecting quickly, hoping to soften the blow, said, "Well, not *that* bad."

My other sister, chastening my mother, and crying, said, "Yes it *is,* Mom!"

It's funny but my mother and my chastening sister were both right in their separate ways. My sister, of course, meant -- Jeanne is his friend, *our* friend, our families *know* each other, she died with calamitous sudden-ness, you can't say it's "not *that* bad". My mother certainly didn't mean "it's not that bad" in an eye-rolling "toughen-up, butter cup" kind of way. She certainly meant (This was in late May of 1994. My brother Brian had died some half a year earlier. Everything was death. And every death seemed to shrink in terror of my brother's awful departure.) compared to losing your brother, to losing my son, compared to the devastation we endured just a walk-around-the-block-ago. She didn't mean "it's not *that* bad". She meant "it's not THAT".

Meanwhile, I, stone-faced and prepared for the inevitability of death, stood at the entrance of my home, with the door just closed a second ago behind me, and waited. In fact, I expected, as they fumbled with their telling of the terrible news, to learn that another brother of mine might have died, perhaps in a car wreck or some other fatal accident.

"Jeanne died," someone said.

I can't remember who actually said it. Do you believe that? I can remember where everyone was sitting. I can remember everything up until the actual announcement. I was elsewhere. I don't know where. I was spinning somewhere. I was cradling my broken heart somewhere, lulling it to sleep with soothing lullabies, imploring myself from the deep nooks and crannies of hurt to breathe, just breathe, just breathe, move, just move, walk, DON'T talk, blink, don't cry, don't fall don't fall don't fall don't fall this is death this is just death this is life this is just life this is the way it happens. Breathe.

Some months ago, when talking to my sister about the little touch of loss and its impact on my life and my need to write about all that's happened, I mentioned these deaths of friends and loved ones. In order of disappearance: Frank (a strange sad ripple, a foreshock), Brian (the annihilation), Jeanne Marie (numbness), Doug (I was a confused, wann-be-adult), Tommy (*again*?), Sophia (my baby my heart my heart my aching heart how much more must I endure?)

My sister said, "That's a lot." And she repeated after a second of consideration, "That's a lot."

And I agreed and said, "It is."

It is a lot.

Lashing Out

This is difficult for me to sort through, or to admit, but lashing out at unsuspecting and innocent people is a bit of a specialty of mine. But there are a few occasions on which I know that my attacking the world was a symptom of my being completely lost. A symptom that I ascribed, incorrectly, to my loss.

Captain Ahab, a classic desperado, says to Starbuck, "That inscrutable thing is chiefly what I hate; and be the white whale agent, or be the white whale principal, I will wreak that hate upon him. Talk not to me of blasphemy, man; I'd strike the sun if it insulted me."

Losing Sophia is the inscrutable world flexing its muscle. And I will wreak my hate upon it. I would strike the sun if it insulted me. I've always loved that line because I knew what Ahab felt. He was pained and harmed and abused by the world. And he would get it back, goddammit! I will get my vengeance. I'll show *you*, WORLD!

And so I lash out.

I need not tell anyone this, but lashing out has everything to do with the pain I've been caused, but at the same time—and more importantly, more *frequently*—has nothing to do with the pain I've been caused.

My dry cleaner lost a suit of mine. It was a black suit. It was still in the plastic when I went to put it on one day after I'd picked it up from the cleaner.

I thought, "Holy hell, did I gain weight in a *week*?" I could barely pull the waist button closed. I took off the pants and looked at the blazer. Now I know that not all black fabrics are the same, especially when it comes to a suit. I noticed that the stitch was different also.

I looked at the tag. Yep. Different suit.

I went back to the cleaner, who was a friendly guy, to tell him what happened. He made me try the suit on. Right there. In front of him. For real, bro?

I was offended that he wouldn't take my word for it. The customer is always right, right? And if not the customer, then *I* am always right! *Right*?

When I exited the dressing room, he said with a shrug, "It fits."

His laundry girl, at the counter next to him, said, "Barely."

I said, "C'mon, man. *Really*? It's not my suit. Why would I do that? You lost it and you tried to give me some cheap suit to replace it. You owe me money, man."

He said, "no" and it didn't go so well from there. I left in a huff.

Don't worry. I'm just getting warmed up.

A couple days later, he called me and said he felt bad and he'd give me a check to replace the suit. Ok good. When I went over to get the check, he was out. His wife was there. She said she didn't know anything about it.

Oh boy. Mikey's getting *angry*.

I said, "Call him."

"Now?"

"Now."

When she hung up, she said that he said he's not paying for it.

I flipped out. On the *wife*! Completely nuts. Someone called the police. Four patrol cars showed up. The cops were cool enough, but when one cop grabbed me by the elbow to guide me to the door, I said, "Don't touch me. I'll go outside.

Just don't touch me." The way I remember it, he went for his stick, but another officer kinda put his hand up and said, "Ok. Just go outside." They brought me outside.

When we went out, one of the officers said that I said, "I'm gonna come back for him. Tell him to watch his ass," and that that kind of a threat could be "construed" (he used the word construed) as assault, an arrestable offense. I almost wanted to say fuck it. Arrest me. I'll strike the sun. I was outside my mind. It was out of hand.

I spoke to the owner a couple days later on the phone. He said he thought of pressing charges, but then he realized he shouldn't have changed his mind like that. He apologized. That *really* made me feel like garbage. He said he would reimburse me for the suit. I declined. I told him I was terribly wrong. I felt awful, and I might never forgive myself for the way I behaved. I hoped someday he and his wife might forgive me. As if that weren't a terrible enough feeling, he said, "Mike, I know you lost a baby. And I'm sorry. But you're a nice guy. I hope you can find peace."

Peace. Find peace. My eyes welled up and my heart ached. I clenched my teeth and squeaked out a "Thanks." I hung up the phone and sobbed.

Peace. The thing, I think, is that at my worst, though I want to return to the world the pain it has inflicted on me, when I behave in ways like this I am ashamed to betray what I feel has always been a more natural sense of compassion and gentleness in my heart. In the end—I think I just want peace. In my heart. But how could I find peace in my heart when my heart was in shambles? When my heart was so lost?

What made me so emotional when the Dry Cleaner wished me peace was his articulation of a truth about myself that I was ignoring. Or a truth about myself I had lost.

And that lack of self-awareness is frustrating, it's upsetting. But it's more than that. It's still hard to speak truthfully about loss, but the point is that I lashed out. I struck the sun, so to speak. And in my mind, at the time, I did it because "I'm angry" about losing my baby. I held my lifeless daughter. Do you know how that felt for me? I'm not talking emotionally right now. I mean physically. Do you know what that felt like *physically?* Like a bag of apples. That's what she felt like. Pick up your child. Feel the warmth and life and joy and future. Feel the love. The tears. The giggles. Feel the hope and heartbreak. The success and failure. Feel the graduations and weddings. The first homes and first words. *I* felt a loss of *life* when I held Sophia. I felt *lifelessness.* Like a bag of apples. I was angry and I want people to know because I'm angry and I wanted to smash something! I wanted people to know.

But, the Dry Cleaner *did* know. He *did* know I'd lost Sophia. He must have heard about our loss from a neighbor or something. Or maybe he saw Tara pick up the cleaning one day and did the math. Or maybe Tara and I *told* him. I can't remember. And I don't know if I realized at the time, but he knew. Maybe he prayed for me and Tara. Maybe he thought of us. Maybe he thought of his own kids. Maybe *he* lost a baby too. But while I made a tantrum-throwing fool of myself, he thought of my baby. When he wished me peace, I realized how wrong I was. About everything. I realized that Sophia couldn't be proud of a Daddy who was so mean to someone, of a Daddy who *thought* of *her* and *acted* like *that.*

I'm sad. But I can't blame my anger on Sophia anymore. I shouldn't be manifesting my sadness as anger at *all*, but certainly not the sadness of Sophia. I needed to find a better expression of my memory of her.

I never spoke to the Dry Cleaner again. I think his name was Alan. I hope he's well.

Kindness

Some of my colleagues delivered some food catered from a local deli to our apartment in Long Beach. Baked ziti, bread, cold cuts and stuff. Chris, a science teacher, a friend of mine and a colleague, rang my apartment. Tara scurried into our bedroom. Chris brought in the food and we chatted for a minute. He may have been the first person other than family that I spoke to after we lost the baby.

We all reach out to each other. Some more so than others. Some resist more than others. Chris was that kind of a guy. He was friendly, always smiling. I'll always remember his bringing food to us that night. I know a bunch of people chipped in, but he brought it. I think there's a certain amount of bravery needed to reach out like that. Simply put, Chris needed to consider that the necessity of a kind gesture must outweigh any discomfort Tara and I, or *he* for that matter, might experience by crossing the threshold of the bereaved. Funeral parlors exist to mitigate this very discomfort. Chris came into our home. He said, in so many words, "I'm here. To let you know I, we, your friends at work, care." The gesture at the time may not always be received, but it has a long shelf life.

After eating that deli order for several days, all of the salty food, I'm sure, bloated and dehydrated us. Somebody sent us an Edible Arrangements. That was the sweetest fruit I ever ate. Tara and I still talk about it to this day.

A group of our friends sent us a gift certificate for a couple's massage at some spa in Port Washington. We were thankful for it and looked forward to having a chance to use it, but, as I've said before, grievers have little room for self-comfort. I can assure you, if someone had sent Tara and me a gift certificate for a public flogging, we would have sprinted to the town square to redeem it.

But sometime later, I was called out from under the rock of grief by my friend Mark (the same one that called me out from bed to meet Tara on that night in LBI back in 1999) to ask if we'd received the gift certificate in the mail. I said we had and that I was sorry to not have thanked him, but it was just...and he cut me off. He wasn't looking for an apology. He said I had nothing to apologize for. He just wanted to make sure it hadn't gotten lost in the mail. I'm sure he just wanted to call actually. I'm sure lots of people just wanted to call.

That is very much the confusion of grief. Wanting everyone to call and wanting everyone to leave me alone at the same time. And the confusion isn't only mine and Tara's: the confusion belongs, as well, to those around the grief-ridden.

Tara and I snuck around our apartment building hoping to avoid contact with anyone in those days. Embarrassment and shame are tough symptoms of grief to shed. One day our neighbor across the hall bumped into us in the elevator. I wish I remembered their names. Innocently enough the wife asked how's the baby. Tara shrank. I put my arm around her and simply looked at our neighbor and shook my head. She put her hand over her mouth and said oh no and started to cry right there in the elevator with us. I remember her offering help of one kind or another. She was a nurse. I don't know where. I don't know what type of nurse she was. But she was a kind woman.

My sister Deirdre was teaching in Ecuador at the time. She came home for the funeral. Then she returned home again a few weeks later for the holidays. She told me she had been mugged in Ecuador a few weeks before—just when we'd lost the baby. I was shocked and disturbed. She's my little sister and her working in Ecuador, while I understood to be a unique opportunity, still troubled me. I asked her why she didn't tell me. Of course, it was a stupid question, I don't know why I even asked. She didn't want to bother me at that time. She said I'd had enough to worry about.

Sometime later that year, a student of mine approached me after class. "Hi Mr. Flood." She handed me a small, neat package. "My Mom runs a bereavement group at St. Kilian's in Farmingdale. She thought you might like this."

The young lady's name was Chrissy Weiss. I looked at the contents of the package and thought to myself, "Oh boy. This is gonna be tough."

Later that day, it was probably Easter or later by then, Tara and I looked through the items. There were various infant loss awareness articles, flower bulbs, personal testimonies and prayers, infant loss bracelets and such. We were by then aware of a community of parents who'd lost infants or pregnancies. It's a larger community than you might think. You probably know someone in this community. You may not *know* you know one. That's a trademark of this community. We're silent. We bereaved parents lack the pride with which some say they are cancer survivors or suffering with cancer. MS. HIV/AIDS (that's come a long way though). ALS. And so on and so on.

But by and large, we suffer our loss silently. Embarrassed. Ashamed. Or even worse, "conscientious"—you know, we don't want to spoil the party. We don't want to be the "Debbie Downer." That's an easy way to ruin a conversation—tell someone you're grieving an infant death or stillbirth. Yeah, we're a buzzkill.

Chrissy's mom is Martha Weiss. *She* should be writing a book! She has experienced some devastation, for sure. When

Tara and I went through the contents of that package, we realized my student's mom, Martha Weiss, was actually a name we'd heard before through the bereavement group grapevine. Friends of ours, Brian and Kathleen Sullivan, attended a monthly healing session at St. Kilian's in Farmingdale, New York. Martha ran the group. They spoke very highly of "this woman," Martha. At the time we didn't know her and I hadn't realized that Chrissy, my student at the time, was her daughter. I'd meet Martha some years later, in what Martha would call a "provident accident."[2] Martha Weiss

---

[2] Meeting Martha Weiss. I thought this story was too long to fit in the text, but too good to ignore. Here's to provident accidents, Martha!

I was trying to find Martha Weiss for some time. I wanted to tell her about our annual Toy Drive in memory of Sophia. I knew Martha had a bereavement group at St. Kilian's in Farmingdale, and I was hoping maybe she could spread the word for our Drive.

In any case, I'm an idiot, and I was searching around for NANCY Weiss. Calling phone numbers and messaging emails for people named NANCY Weiss. What a dope!

On the Wednesday afternoon before Thanksgiving of 2016, the high school at which I teach hosts a first year alumni Mass and brunch. Literally dozens and dozens if not hundreds of first year grads come back to their beloved high school to see mugs like me (or to show us that their hair is purple).

I was stationed in my position as a cafeteria moderator sixth period when a former student of mine, accompanied by another grad whom I'd never taught, came up to say hello. We chatted about college for a few minutes, and as we said farewell, I glanced at her companion's name tag: Hello, my name is... Tim Weiss.

I looked at the young man, and said by the way, your mom's not NANCY Weiss, is she?

"No, sorry," he said regretfully, "her name is Martha."

"Martha!" I laughed aloud and told him I'd been looking for his mom for weeks and told him of my mixing up her name. We talked for several minutes. I told him of our connection. He assured me she would love to get in touch. And she did. And just two weeks later Martha came to our Toy Drive as she promised. Martha and I have become friends since then. She's come to the Sophia Michelle Toy Drive for a few years now, and I

must be one of the most caring people I know. And I'm willing to bet that she'll say she coped with her suffering and loss by reaching out to others. Oh, and by giving out kick-ass hugs. Those are some good hugs, Martha.

What makes some people reach out and some people withdraw? What makes people think I'm going to do something kind to let the world know I'm here? When an occasion calls for kindness, some withdraw. Others reach out. Some think about it and convince themselves to reach out or to withdraw. For others, it's a reflex. How is the behavior determined?

In October of 2016, Ivy Diamond (speaking of good people), the director of the Child Loss Bereavement Program at Northshore/Long Island-Jewish Hospital, contacted me and asked if I'd consider sharing Sophia's memory at the annual Memorial Service sponsored by her program. While I was delivering my talk at the podium in the conference room, I was struggling through a particular memory. I had rehearsed the speech so many times that the night before the service I was reading it without tears. (While I was proud of myself for "getting over" the emotion of telling our story, a part of me was disappointed in myself: I thought, "If I don't cry, people won't know how sad this has made me. If I don't cry, will Sophia think I don't care anymore?").

But there, in the midst of the speech, I was losing the battle of not crying. I pinched my eyes shut tight, placed my finger and thumb to the bridge of my nose, and tried to collect myself. I wasn't sure if I would be able to. I grew nervous that midway through this remembrance of my baby I would have to stop. I looked up, tried to re-establish control of my

---

delivered a talk on loss and healing at her GAPS event at St. Kilian's. Martha's an incredible, selfless, faithful, positive woman. I'm glad I stumbled across Tim that day. And I'm glad I had Chrissy in class all those years ago.

quivering lip, and saw someone walking up the far-right aisle. He was an old man. Gray hair and sun beaten skin. He was dressed in a well-worn Oxford and dungarees. He walked slowly to the podium. I didn't know who he was or what he was doing. Honestly, I think I thought of asking, "What the hell are you *doing*?"

Maybe he's just going to a different seat.

Maybe he's leaving through a different exit.

Is he some nut who's going to attack me or worse, shoot the place up?

No.

He came slowly to the podium, I looked at him....he handed me a tissue. A tissue. For my tears.

He said nothing. He turned around and walked back to his seat.

I wiped my eyes and nose and finished talking about my baby.

What made him perform that act of kindness: human decency? a lifelong commitment to courtesy? compassion?.....*love*?

I wish I had gotten a chance to know him afterwards. Or even learned his name. But maybe I guess I know him well enough. He cared. He helped. How much better could I ever hope to know a stranger?

These little kindnesses have a big impact. They help. They help restore faith in the world. It's not all sadness. I don't have to be ashamed. Or embarrassed. Sad? Yeah sure there's nothing "wrong" with being sad, but it's ok for me to feel good too. That probably seems obvious, but after the trauma of seeing the birth of my lifeless child, holding my lifeless child, kissing my lifeless child...well let's just say up is down and down is up. Your entire compass is—frankly—"fucked."

But I'm hoping, nearly ten years later, maybe, my compass is finally pointing true again. I hope.

Camping

I like walking in the woods but I'm always cautious to avoid getting away from a path I know or a clear marker—a stream or ridge or road or rock wall. I go camping in a place in the Catskills region of New York. I think it's a place called Lew Beech, but we've always called it Beaverkill. It's state land, a single lane dirt road in. No electric or running water. No bathrooms. Things like that. I love that place. You could very much get lost there, I think.

When Tara and I got married, she thought going there was a stupid idea because she was afraid that I might get hurt and not be found. Or that something might happen at home and no one would be able to reach me.

I never really thought about it like that. All I know is that it's massively peaceful there. The night sky is still sparkling with stars and galaxies. The quiet and stillness are—pristine. Maybe it's silly but that spot I go to still feels like a place from a time before now.

I love to walk in those woods. I can say the potential for getting lost is real in those woods and it is frightening and being *alone* up there can be terrifying, but generally speaking, walking around those pathless beech and black tupelo trees in the autumn in the fallen leaves along the creek flowing like quicksilver all glistening light and dark in torrents and eddies—*mysterium tremendum*—I think is the experience, the expression of the experience.

My buddies and I went up there once and a new guy came

up for the first time. His name was Jay. Nice guy but, I guess, not much of an outdoorsman, so to speak. We'd been out looking for firewood for a few hours when we thought it was getting cool and time to start a fire and drink some beer.

After a bit, one of the guys wondered aloud, "Where's Jay?"

Oh shoot. Jay.

We called out. No answer. After a few minutes of a local calling and searching, we stood quietly, assessing in our private thoughts the chance of someone being catastrophically injured. It was, in my experience anyway, a moment of vulnerability not usually sensed with that particular group of guys.

But there it was, a very faint call for help. We broke into four directions—it was hard to pinpoint the location of the cry because its faintness and the terrain made it seem as though it were coming from everywhere and nowhere at once. We called to him in synchrony so to more clearly hear if he were responding to us or just yelling for help. Most frightening for me at the time was whether he was just calling out to locate us or crying out in pain. I imagined the ordeal of finding him with a broken leg or worse and us fools drunkenly humping his ass out on a cockamamie litter.

But we were getting closer. And as we got closer, I heard him calling out again and again "I'm here. I'm right here." How odd to say I'm right here but have no idea where right here actually is. He was sitting on a downed tree. He was panicked when we found him and we busted him for that of course, because, you know, we were such mountain men and all, but the truth is that I was scared too and I've been turned around and disoriented in that place before. He said he thought he was gonna die. He knew it was getting dark and he heard the coyotes the night before and he was only wearing jeans and a T-shirt and he thought he might die of hypothermia. We laughed at him and walked him back to the site and it was dark by then, so he sat by the fire and drank a beer. Probably lots of beer. We all did. And he didn't leave the fire for the rest of the night. But that was really scary.

By time Tara and I had Charlotte, our first child after Sophia, I had gone to Beaverkill more seldom. But one year, when I decided to go up with a few of the guys, Tara told me I needed to tell her *exactly* where this place is, *exactly* how to get there.

So, I wrote the directions down, but I was curious, so I went to Google Earth and I found that needle in the haystack of the Catskills. It was cool. There's lots of little-known gems in the wilderness around that spot in Beaverkill. Google Earth is amazing. I could look at it for hours. Maps or globes in general really. Anyway, I wrote the coordinates down and left them with Tara.

Ostensibly, I did this so that Tara would know where I was, but why? Why did she need to know where I was? Why would she need to find me? Of course, my knuckle-headed buddies surmised it was the old ball and chain, but that couldn't be further from the truth. Tara wanted to know where I was in case of tragedy, of course. In case something awful might happen again. In case that one in a trillion space rock came flying from the cosmos and landed in my little baby's crib while I was off carousing in the woods, Tara would be able to find me.

Wanting to know where *everything* is *all* the time has been an unexpected result of the trauma of infant loss.

I have dreams about Beaverkill sometimes. They're anxiety dreams. Some looming, indistinct danger. Very often, the anxiety of these dreams originates in the presence of dream strangers. They're either camping nearby or driving around, circling my space. Once there was a monster. It was in the woods. I had no idea what it looked like. I never actually saw it. But I thought, in the dream, it might look like

Gossamer from the Loonie Tunes, in his "horrifying" moments. I was in terror throughout the dream as I tried to get to the car and the campsite, and the supplies and a fire started and all along this monstrousness is in the woods.

I don't know what that means. Having dreams like that. I'm telling you that that Beaverkill spot is one of my favorite places in the world. Why would such a special place in my life manifest itself so regularly as a nightmare?

Maybe it's because I go to Beaverkill to *feel* lost. To *get* lost so to speak. To get away from this place—whatever this place might be at any given time. Or that's what it started as. Going up there with the "boys" with a can of soup and a case of beer. The sense of being haunted in those dreams, I wonder, might be my subconscious wagging its finger at me for "avoiding." In other words, the very place itself is haunting me in my dreams because of my motivation for being there. Put another way, if I am so averse to being lost, why would I go somewhere to *get* lost? Why would I want something that I fear? I think the sinners' joy at the River Acheron in Dante is described by Virgil as their *desire* for the thing they *fear*. I guess I'm wondering if I went up to Beaverkill, instead, to truly find peace, to write or walk or fish or explore, I might find truth. Peace. Maybe then I would be able to go to Beaverkill to *find* myself rather than to get lost. Maybe if I went up there for that reason rather than for escape, maybe I wouldn't dream about it like I do.

A-camping we will go! Beaverkill, NY. That's me to the left. I always loved going out in the woods!

The Cemetery

Sophia is buried at St. Charles Resurrection Cemetery. My brother Brian is buried there also. But Sophia, along with so many other tragically departed children, is buried in the Holy Innocence section. It's a strange place in a certain respect. The absolute saddest loss a parent can experience, the type of loss that *everyone* winces at, is concentrated in a few thousand square feet of death. But the strange part is that so many of the children's grave markers (marble stones with bronze plates) are adorned with stuffed animals, Tonka trucks, various toys, bats and balls, balloons, and such. Some have nothing. I wonder at all of the markers. The names. The ages. The sweet messages of devastated parents printed on the plates. The siblings. How many parents have suffered multiple losses? How many sets of twins? It's preposterously sad. But something about the toys has always had a strange effect on me. They helped. I would go there with Tara and sometimes we'd sit for hours. We'd arrange stuffed animals and balloons and flowers for Sophia. We'd say hello to Sophia's neighbors. Formisano. Kelleher. We'd talk to her. We'd say a few prayers. But after a while, it made me feel happy to get there. In a way I guess I felt like I was Daddy taking care of my little girl. And the other children at Holy Innocents were Sophia's friends. Seeing all those grave sites with all those toys...I don't know. A little playground for the dead. A nursery for the spirit angels. A statue of Christ holding a child is in the center of Holy Innocents. It reads, "The Lord is the keeper of little children."

Tara and I went every Saturday. Or every weekend anyway. For years, really. In the winter months and the shortening days, we placed solar lights at her marker (so many others did the same) so she wouldn't be afraid of the dark. If we went away for the weekend, we'd ask someone in the family to visit, to pull the weeds around the marker, replace the dying flowers in the green pvc vase with fresh ones, straighten up the arrangement of her toys, to make this departed child's place look like a place of love. It's a difficult task and not for the faint of heart.

For her birthday each year, we "celebrated" on December 5 at Sophia's site. We would decorate. Buy her a stuffed animal. And we would take pictures of ourselves in front of the grave with balloons anchored to the earth beside Sophia's marker, hoping the joy might not float away. Each year from a florist in Seaford called Flower Barn, we ordered a floral arrangement that resembled a birthday cake. It was a pink masterpiece. All little girls with butterflies and sparkles and such. Two men, Murray and Mike, owned it. The first time we picked up the arrangement, I cried. I don't know if Mike knew what he did for me and how important it was, but he learned for sure, and he made that arrangement for a few years until he sold the business. He was a sweet guy.

In the first spring, when we went to visit Sophia, we were horrified. The grass and earth before her marker had been dug up and disrupted. Just a few weeks earlier we were elated by the growing grass and flowers we'd planted. It was life. The value of that could be lost on *no one*. But here we were staring at what I really thought was the desecrated grave of my baby daughter, who had *nothing*, of whom I had so little, for whom this little cemetery plot with dirt and grass and stone and stuffed toys was *everything*. I surveyed the scene and realized a new plot had been dug a row or two away. It appeared that the St. Charles crew must have used a machine to dig. The machine devastated my daughter's site. We were so hurt. It was like another death. We called the office and the crew came out. They were sympathetic and promised to have the director call. He did. I explained my feelings.

He said, "Mr. Flood, I buried my son last week. I'm not saying this for your pity. I'm just telling you I understand. I will personally take care of your daughter's space." And he did.

It's amazing to me the stories of loss that are behind so many faces. The long stories of sadness beneath every grave. I wish I had asked him about his son. I wish I wasn't always so wrapped up in my own loss. Or so sensitive to others' desire (real or imagined) for privacy.

We used to blow bubbles there. For some reason it became a thing. I don't know why or what made it a thing, but we would blow bubbles every week. At first Tara and I thought that maybe it was insensitive. Doing something "fun" at such a somber place. But we saw all the toys around. All the stuffed animals. And then we saw that when people arrived and saw our bubbles floating over all the graves, over the heads of all the stuffed toys, maybe they smiled sometimes.

Learning it was ok to smile. Learning that Sophia's life could be a joy in some ways. That was important. I think I was recognizing something positive could be taken. I'm certain I *said* as much right after she died, but it took some years of little tiny impacts and adjustments, influences and insights (our own and others'), kindnesses, smiles, and memories, before I really *understood* that Sophia, and it's still hard to say this or believe it, but Sophia is a *good* part of my life. I feel like Holy Innocents had a lot to do with that discovery.

Happy Birthday, Sophia! Tara and I celebrating our baby's birthday at Holy Innocents in St. Charles-Resurrection Cemetery.

Christmas Eve Mass, December 2008

Just a few weeks after Sophia was born still, Tara and I went to Midnight Mass for Christmas Eve at St. Mary of the Isle in Long Beach. Just a few weeks before, we had Sophia's Funeral. The celebrant, I think his name was Fr. Chris, had just a few weeks before said her funeral Mass and just a day or two earlier than that visited our home to say a prayer with us.

He gave me a somber nod as he processed in.

His homily was about hope.

As he ended his homily, he said, "Maybe you've lost something. Maybe someone is ill. Maybe a loved one has died."

He paused. "Maybe you've suffered the death of an infant."

He concluded, "There's hope. Christmas is hope."

He was talking to us, I was certain. Or if he didn't intend to, he did so anyway.

As Mass ended, I was sitting on the aisle, the priest processed out, and when he was about to pass me, he slowed, looked at me, shook my hand and mouthed clearly to me, "Thank you."

I wondered for what, but I'm sure I had a feeling I knew for what. For being here, maybe? For not having anger towards God? (I did, of course, have anger towards God, but something compelled Tara and me to go to church anyway.) For celebrating! I'm certain priests feel church attendance very personally. And I don't know if some of them are discouraged by low attendance, but I would bet all of them are glad and thankful for any and all that do attend. Maybe our presence there encouraged him. Maybe he had doubts about the healing strength of God or the spirit of humankind or whatever. Maybe he saw us there and said "Yes! Thank you, God!" It was like, maybe, he was saying thank you for coming to his party on the happiest celebration of the year, like he was saying, "Thank you for taking time out of your schedule to be here on Christmas Eve."

I certainly perceived that he was acknowledging our loss, also. It was a "'Thanks for coming' even though I know how bad you're hurting right now, how much you think your prayers failed you, how much your attendance at church did *nothing* for you, how much the *Church* or your *faith* failed you, how much *God* failed you....Thanks for coming because somehow, I'm willing to bet, we *both* know that the help you're looking for is still *here.* In Church. With these parishioners and all of their pains and losses and sorrows. The abandonment you feel is helped here. Thank you for being with us."

No matter what, that "thank you" made me feel strong and proud.

My Compass

I love orienteering. Or I should say I love *people* that know how to orienteer. *I* don't know how to orienteer. I love survivalists. I love people that can go out and trek and just manage. They always know where they are. They're probably such great problem solvers. Or maybe things just never become problematic because they are always so centered that stressors don't register. Nothing panics them. They never have anxiety.

I have a beautiful compass. My wife bought it for me. I haven't the *foggiest* idea of how to use it though. But it is *really nice*. All of the numbered and lined exactitude contained in the sturdy case. And I can look at it and spin in circles always amazed by its ability to point north, in spite of my own dizziness. I *wish* I knew how to use it, but I wouldn't even know how to start.

My daughter Charlotte just gave to me for Father's Day this year a compass on a carabiner clip. It doesn't exactly work, which makes me a little sad, but I cherished the thought, and what the little compass means, whether or not she knows what it means to me.

In any case, I don't know why she bought it for me. She definitely thought about it, though. She's a thoughtful kid. She bought it at a little school fair. Tara said she walked around holding a couple of items and deliberating. I don't know if she knew that Tara bought me a compass and maybe she thought I should have a compass from *all* of the women I love in my life (which of course, I should) or why she should buy me a compass for Father's Day, but it hit the spot, for sure.

But I buckled the bright green-chrome carabiner to my work bag, and I told Charlotte, "Now I'll always know what direction to go."

"So, you'll always know how to get home," she said, with the holy wisdom only a child can have.

"Where are You?"

"Where are you, Sophia?"

I say it aloud. I'm in a car. In my basement. In the yard, mowing the lawn, sitting in my Adirondack chair, looking at my whole life.

"I'm looking for signs. I see a bird and I think of you. I think of you every day. I see the name *Sophia* and I think of you. Sophia Coppola is one of my favorite directors *because* her name is Sophia! (And she looks a little like Mommy, too!)

"Where are you, Sophia? I look for you in flying kites and balloons, floating bubbles from the joyfully colored wands and the gleeful shouts of kids that I wish you'd grown to know. I look for you in flocks of birds and angel wings. Where are you, Sophia?"

Where are you, Sophia? Where are you?

Sophia's Funeral

Why didn't we announce our baby's funeral? Why didn't we ask anyone to attend?

The death of a child exists in a fortress of shame. The turrets are high. The moat is deep. It's a castle of horrors where the only life is the life of the bereaved parents and we are inquisitor and inquisitioned, torturer and tortured, executioner and executed, and moaning masses alike.

The castle keeps everyone out. I don't know who built the castle. Did I and Tara? Did a world of ignorance force us to? Or did that world build it for us—to keep us and our pain contained, more prison-like than castle? Maybe, then, it is we bereaved, too, who have built the prison.

Only my parents and Tara's, siblings and in-laws were at the funeral. It's important for me to think about this.

In some ways, I remember thinking, I was afraid no one would come. What if someone didn't come? Would I think that that person didn't accept my daughter as a life? Or at least as a part of my life and Tara's? So when whoever didn't come attempted to explain why, I would be forced to say, "Oh, yeah, no problem. I understand." Or I'd lash out. We know how that goes.

But I've known for a long time now, that this didn't really have anything to do with anyone else—or maybe it's got everything to do with everyone else. No matter why I thought what I thought, at that time or at this time, or why I did what I did, I did it because I was afraid. Afraid of what others would think. I'm afraid my loss and my hurt will somehow be invalidated. I'm afraid others will think I've let my wife down. I didn't protect her. I'm afraid of being ashamed. Maybe I'm just afraid to be so vulnerable.

No matter what, that funeral may have been a "push" away. Somehow, we tacitly requested privacy. That sends a message. So, I've built a fortress and from behind its wall I'm crying out for help and love but all anyone can see is the wall I've built around myself.

No matter what, the only people at the funeral were our parents and siblings. My brother- in-law Marc gave me a hug. He had a tear in his eye. I've never seen him get emotional. Only when he was saying goodbye to his own mother, he spoke at the side of her coffin and cried as he spoke. Tara and I hugged everyone as we saw them inside the church.

I don't remember who it was, but I was trying so hard to keep it together, everyone looked at us with those long faces and teary eyes and the knowing of pain and loss and the wishing it didn't have to happen this way. I don't remember who it was, Jill, my brother Thomas's wife, I think? Maybe it was Denis, my brother. I'm not sure, but I said, "I wanted her so bad," and started to cry. Really cry. And I was hugged.

We processed up the aisle and little Sophia's little shoe box-sized coffin was there and everyone was sobbing and Tara and I were holding each other while holding the little knit hat Sophia wore at birth to keep her warm in the cold of death and I listened to the priest and the platitudes and the never knowing *anything* about what God wants or does.

It's not that it doesn't help. It's not that it *does* help. But it's right to have had a funeral for Sophia. Or, right for me, anyway. I'm glad we did it. Some people don't. And I have heard some say they are sad they didn't, while others are better off without it. But I'm glad we did it. Only because, and this is really the service the church provided I think, because even though we didn't notify anyone of the service, the cantor was there. It's not the priest (through no real fault of his own) but the cantor that made an impression on me.

As he stood at the lectern, he sang "You Are Mine" (yes, if you've ever been to church you know the one. It makes *everyone* cry—"Do not be afraid, I am with you, I have called you each by name...." Right?) And as he sang, he cried. The cantor cried!

And that's why having a funeral was right for me. Whether it was I who didn't want anyone there, or others who wouldn't have come, the cantor, the church, that *song* made me feel *not alone*. Maybe you don't need the church to do that. Maybe you might think I *shouldn't* need the church for that. But in the end, coping with loss has *everything* to do with being "not alone" and being alone has everything to do with never coping.

There's a liturgy I think for loss of a child. The gospel at those Masses, about Jesus rebuking the apostles because they shooed away the children, goes like this:

> "And people were bringing children to him that he might touch them, but the disciples rebuked them. When Jesus saw this he became indignant and said to them, 'Let the children come to me; do not prevent them, for the kingdom of God belongs to such as these. Amen, I say to you, whoever does not accept the kingdom of God like a child will not enter it.' Then he embraced them and blessed them, placing his hands on them."

Maybe some think that a pre-formatted liturgy is less than "authentic" but the fact is those hymns and readings help. The gospel of Jesus and the children is perfect because Jesus was all about accepting those "others" who were typically rejected. And those rejections haven't changed all that much in the last two thousand years. *I* felt rejected. I felt my *baby* was rejected.

That gospel is helpful like Buddhist parables are helpful: You don't have to believe in anything for it to make sense. Sometimes, Jesus—God, Son of God, Prophet, Rebel Street Poet Philosopher—sometimes, he just made sense.

And I felt his message of love when that cantor cried as he sang for my baby at her funeral.

GG Ma

My father's mother's name is Gertrude Rita Flood. I didn't know that was her middle name until after she passed. I suppose that's when we learn quite a bit about the people we know and love. My grandmother was a pretty special person. She maybe wasn't what you would think of as a "grandma" at least not in any sense of the cute and cuddly Hallmark type. She was austere. Wise. She was funny. Rebellious. Grandma Flood, as we were trained to refer to her, conceived eleven children, mothered nine children, grandmothered thirty-two grandchildren, and great-grandmothered some three dozen great grandchildren (I can't say I know exactly how many). Her greatgrandmotherdom is how she came to be monikered GG MA. As far as I was told, when the great grandchildren started to come, someone asked her what she'd like to be called: she chose the abbreviated Great Grand Ma—GG Ma. She was never ordinary. Perhaps traditional, but never ordinary.

I always knew that my dad had siblings that didn't live, that GG Ma had lost babies. It was sad when I heard of it as a child, many many decades after it had happened, but it was also awe-inspiring, that she had *eleven* children. There was a heroism in that abundance of offspring that I thought I could (or should) be proud of. Nine was a lot, but eleven? *That* was epic. I never knew how they died or what happened, but they died as babies, as far as I understood. I never asked, and no one ever really told me. Probably for many of the same reasons I refer to my *two* children, my dad and his siblings grew up talking about the nine children in *their* family.

But when Tara and I lost Sophia, GG Ma, in very uncharacteristic fashion, shared with me her history of child loss.

I wish I could recall the date of this particular conversation. And it's not that the date is important, but I have no *idea* when it was. Was it shortly after Sophia died or was it months?

Anyway, GG Ma told me that she'd lost two babies. I loved talking to her. There was always some nugget of controversy, some surprising shock or subversion or scandal. But she was sitting in her chair with the afghan (she probably made it) that she always had (was it brown and white and green—I wonder where that afghan is now) over her knees, and she told me about her losses. Of one loss she told me that the nurse said oh my god when she first saw the baby. GG ma never even got to see the child. The lifeless babe was whisked away. When GG Ma asked to see her child, the doctor said no. She told me that she caught a glimpse: the child's skull was only partially formed. I can't really imagine it.

GG Ma told me that she'd brought up the child's demise to my Grandfather sometime after the loss, and he simply and sternly and definitively forever said, "No! We won't talk about this." And I can see that happening, not because of any fault in my grandfather's character, but because of my own disinclination to talk, or my father's or any and every man's.

No doubt we're coming around, gents, right? You don't get to listen to Robert Smith sing "Boys Don't Cry" and not realize the irony of it. Culturally, we are, hopefully, emerging from the dark ages of masculinity, but I know my grandfather's disinclination to talk was NOT his individual aversion or his "gender's" aversion, but instead an aversion experienced by most people in the case of a baby's death. I know the resistance and the discomfort—on my part and on the part of others—well.

I'll always remember talking to my grandmother because she said, "Your baby is still with you, Michael. She'll always be with you. She's with the saints and angels now and they are always with us. I know it."

GG Ma has passed now, and I miss her. I wish I could have spoken to her again about her babies, especially now, writing about Sophia, I wish I could have asked her again and paid attention to the details. Though I can't complain. She lived a good long life and I knew her better in my adulthood than I did as a child, and I think that's a lucky thing.

She was in Mercy Hospital in Rockville Centre and she was dying. Someone said something about hospice. GG Ma just wanted to go home. Even if she knew she were going to die, she wanted to be home. But she didn't make it back.

I went to visit her at Mercy after stopping at my parents' in nearby Lybrook. On our way home, I parked the car in the hospital lot and told Tara and my daughter Charlotte that I'd just be a few minutes. I don't know why I thought I'd only be a few minutes. I maybe thought she would get better, or get home, and I'd see her again, or maybe I just thought "what else is there now to do, I'll just say goodbye." I don't have any idea what I thought, or why I thought I'd be a few minutes, but really I wanted to be a few hours or days because, really, I wanted to ask her about every thought she ever had.

So, I visited her room and she was thankfully alertish. She called me by my name. I asked her how she was feeling, and she said fine. She looked weak and frail in this hospital bed and not in her chair at home with a book nearby and her sweater and her tissue folded into her sleeve "just in case." She was thin and gray-skinned and she looked dry— like she was thirsty but couldn't think of anything any longer that might quench her thirst. Her cup overflowed. She believed that. She *said* that. I'm thinking she knew she was going to meet God.

But when it was time to leave, I said goodbye to her that night, I hugged her and I didn't know if I should do that because she wasn't the affectionate type and a little kiss on the cheek was usually sufficient but I knew she loved me and I hugged her because I knew she was dying and I said in the familiar way, "bye Grandma, I'll see you tomorrow" even though I knew that was probably a lie and I wouldn't see her tomorrow but I said I'd see her tomorrow, anyway.

Then I added, "I love you" and she must have known then that I knew it was the end because I never said that since I was old enough to know what I was saying. I'm not sure if she knew I loved her or if she knew she were dying, but really I'm not sure I ever knew what she knew because what she knew was so beyond me. It was in me and from me and for me and for all of her numerous offspring and her offsprings' offspring and their offspring too and the countless people she knew and affected and influenced and tutored and, like contours on the topographical map of her life that radiate in concentric waves around the peak of her mountain-soul, moved a good hand or gesture or deed six or seventy degrees of separation from her. Her knowledge originated in the divinity of the human spirit and it was disciplined and love and and and *faith*, my God! I couldn't *begin* to know what she knew!

I left GG Ma and I walked down to the car where Tara and Charlotte were waiting. I should have just told Tara to go home so I could wait to see my grandmother die, like I maybe owed her to do, but I also owed it to be with Tara and to be with the baby sister of a baby that never lived to see the light of day. I owed it to them to never miss anything I could help missing because I missed everything of Sophia. So I owed it to them too.

When I got in the car, Tara asked me how GG Ma was and I think I just said, "I think she's ok."

She died that night.

The way I remember hearing it, she was alone when she died and that hurt to hear when I heard it but I should have known better: GG Ma was never alone. She was too full of the spirit of her family to ever be alone. She was too full of the Lord's spirit to ever be alone. My dad says he thinks she was "ready" to die, that she was at peace with her good life and at peace with God and the world. Knowing GG Ma, I'm sure my dad was probably right, but there's got to be a moment of panic or terror before the final breath for just about everybody. No?

No. I don't want to hear that. I hope for someone to tell me I'm wrong, to tell me there are some people who really know it's all ok, even at death, into the *unknown* and *unknowable* and *always* death, to tell me there are people like John Donne who believed in the power of the human soul, who, *even at death*, still might have believed everything he said about the power of the soul, to tell me that someone like Brian Doyle and his "big honkin' brain tumor" still saw, at his last breath, all the same light and love and still believed in death the way he believed in life—tell me they exist, *please*!

Because—if they do—I'll feel so much better about Sophia. And about the day I die.

Grandma Flood, GG Ma, Mama, Mrs. Flood, one of the most impactful people I've ever known.

Memorials and Remembering

Good lord!! I can't remember how everything went! How long did I stay home from work? I must have gone back before Christmas.

Sophia died on December 5. Well actually December 4 but we've always remembered December 5—the day she was delivered. So, Christmas was only 3 weeks later.

I wish I could have done a better job of remembering the sorrow. We have photographers and videographers at all of the happy events. Why not at the sad events? I'd watch a video of a funeral. I'd watch a video of those weeks after Sophia. I read obits and in memoriams in the paper. And I know I'm not the only one. I'd watch a video of me and Tara in our apartment those days. I re-read the letters of sympathy we received, so why not watch a video? Sometimes I think I'm a nut because I want to remember that pain. But, I think sometimes, the pain I have of losing my baby is the only thing I have of her. If I forget that pain, I might forget her.

We remember our babies in so many different ways. Sometimes we see how a grieving parent remembers a stillborn or miscarriage or infant loss, and we think, "That's a good idea. I think I'll do that."

Tara and I saw a woman on the beach last summer setting up candle balloons. It's funny but I think I have a sense for sufferers. I suspected the woman was memorializing someone. Tara asked the woman what she was doing. They talked for a bit and Tara told me that the woman's sister lost a baby and that people were meeting at the beach to send these candle balloons out to the sky above the sea. We didn't stay long enough to see it, but it must have been very impressive. I think I'll do that.

I have a tattoo on my forearm. It reads, "'Sophia Michelle—I have written your name.' Is. 49:16."

I have a black bracelet with a silver plate that reads, "Sophia, my heart." It's actually the second one. The first one was made of black leather. The buckle broke. I keep it in our box of Sophia memories.

Tara has various pieces of jewelry to remember Sophia.

We've had a dove release for Sophia's one-year remembrance.

We have a brick in her name at a hospital.

We've lit candles for Sophia on countless occasions. The first candle we lit for Sophia was right after she died. It may have been that weekend, really. But it was fast. We heard about a church in Queens that has an annual memorial service for departed children. We were still reeling. We needed something to hold onto. We went there and sat for the service and we heard her name—Sophia Michelle—in the candle lit church in the sobbing-sniffling-only quiet church, we heard her name for the first time from someone else's mouth. We cried hard there in that pew. Like so many other people there. Everyone knows your pain.

There's comfort in memorializing. The remembering is painful for some—for all of us—but there's comfort too. Some people just want to forget. At times, I'm sure I just wanted to forget.

I had a student a long time ago. His dad died in the Towers on September 11 some years before I had him in class. He was having a really difficult time. His mom got remarried a year or two after 9-11 and they changed the boy's last name to the new husband's. I don't know how my student felt about that. But sometimes it seems like erasing the memory erases the pain. But I don't know.

One day she called me and asked for a meeting because her son's grades were low. When we met, she talked about his study habits. His work ethic. The time he spends on this or that device or video game. After we exhausted the cliché causes for his lackluster performance and concluded that they were, in fact, symptoms of distress, not reasons for it, I asked her what else she thought might be going on.

She shrugged imperceptibly and shook her head in bafflement, but she eventually got there, even though I could tell she didn't want to recognize or admit or remember it.

"Well, you know my husband, his dad, died on September 11?"

Her lips trembled.

"Yes. I know that."

She looked away from me and tried to control the rush of emotion.

"I don't want to cry," she said.

I shrugged and smiled. "Why not?"

She just clenched her jaw and eyes and shook her head.

"Do you think that might be why he might be avoiding his schoolwork?"

She looked at me, eyes set.

"We have to move on. Everyone does. His life can't stop."

"Of course not."

"He has to get ready for college."

"You're right."

"I'm remarried now, you know."

"Yes. I know. He told me."

She responded, with speed and surprise, "He told you? When? What did he say?"

I suspect she was nervous her son had betrayed her or besmirched her new husband or that maybe he was upset about the second marriage and was adversely affected by it.

"Oh, nothing. You know, 'what's new' type stuff."

"My husband is a good man. He helps me—and my son—in many ways. He's good for us."

"I'm glad for you. That's great news."

She was quiet for a minute.

I took a risk and interrupted the quiet: "My older brother died," I said, "when I was your son's age."

She looked at me and the tears fell freely now.

She asked how he died. I shrugged and said, "It's a long story but he was very ill."

She asked me if it affected me. I told her it did.

She asked, "When does it stop?"

"When does what stop?"

"Hurting."

I think I laughed a short sniffy laugh and said, "Never. Or not so far for me, anyway."

She rolled her head back and rolled her eyes farther and cried some more.

"Do you *want* it to stop? I never thought about it that way. It hurts but it's gotten clearer for me. It gets better. Memories will start to be 'good' after a while. But what happens if it stops? I'm afraid if it stops, I'll forget my brother. I don't want to forget him. And maybe remembering him hurts sometimes, but I can't forget him."

She cried some more, and we didn't say anything for a few minutes.

"I just want him to be ok."

"I know."

We vowed on each of our ends to keep her son working in school. We vowed to motivate him. I don't know what happened. I hope she remembers her husband. I hope he remembers his dad.

I don't ever want to forget Sophia. I do what I can to

remember her.

There's some website called names in the sand or something. Tara and I heard about it from a friend in our bereavement group. As far as I know the story goes, a mother in Australia suffered an infant loss, and to cope and memorialize her child, she wrote the boy's name in the sand and photographed the name against the backdrop of the sand and the waves breaking and the sunset sky. She posted it on this blog or website or whatever it is, and someone saw it and asked her to write the name of her own angel and take a picture and post it. So she did. And she did it again and again until she literally couldn't do it anymore. There were too many babies. Too many names. What a sad cross she bore for all of us. To write the names of our departed babies. To represent a morsel of hope, or despair, for each of us.

I went on there a couple weeks ago. I hadn't been in years really probably seven or more years ago. I visited because I started writing this and I wanted to remember the site and I forgot how powerful it was to see Sophia's name in the sand like that. To see her name at all really, I guess, but when it's represented so beautifully, and publicly—even more, globally—that on the shore of some Australian beach my daughter's name was written in an elegant cursive by someone who didn't know me but knew my pain enough to care and show me how beautiful Sophia could look. It was powerful.

Tara and I, when Sophia's name was first posted on Names in the Sand, were so happy. That's an understatement, but any wording I could choose to describe the feeling would be so understated.

When we checked the website, we saw Sophia's name and breathed a sigh of relief. That it was there, really. A stillborn suspends your trust that *any*thing might come to completion. The mail doesn't come and you feel like the world is coming to an end or is out to get you or you're cursed or something.

When you suffer a stillbirth, you peek out the blinds in the morning unsure if the sun will have risen.

Loved ones can post a message to the name on the website. For a while there, I posted a few messages, and I felt as though I were really talking to her.

So, I went back to Names on the Sand the other day, and I cried like I did the first time because that's what remembering does. Makes it all happen again. And that can be hard. As it is for anyone who suffers with PTSD—remembering can be a nightmare. But remembering can be like hope too, sometimes, I think. It's equal parts the incarceration of *nothing* and the freedom of *everything*.

I went back to the site the other day and remembered the few posts. They were very moving. All longing and loss and dashes of hope. Some love from friends and family—thank you by the way.

Tara and I first posted:

Sophia
Born into Heaven: 12/5/2008
New York

Sophia,
We miss you every day. We wish we could kiss your cheeks. We wish we could rock you to sleep. We wish we could hold you. We wish we could dress you in pretty clothes. We wish we could watch you grow. We will keep your memory with us wherever we go.

Sweet angel,
Mommy and Daddy will love you forever.
Then a friend of ours named Dorie from bereavement posted:
Her name looks so beautiful!!!I knew it was you guys when

you wrote how you wish you could dress her in pretty clothes...I know Sophia is playing with Makayla..

Then Tara's friend Val from work:

Perfect!!!!! She's smiling right back at you guys! God has blessed her with loving parents.
Then my sister Cathleen and brother-in-law Marc
We still cannot believe you are not here with us. Knowing you are in heaven watching over us and your wonderful parents brings us comfort. Send them peace and joy today.

Then I posted a few times:

To my daughter, I see this picture and these words, and think of how much joy you have brought me, even though I never really got to know you. How much joy would you have brought me, if you were with me today?

I love you I love you I love you!

Daddy.

P.S.
Mommy will write you a message too.
Little Birdy, I feel like I am really talking to you when I come to this site. I miss you so much. I love you every second of the day.

Daddy

Sophia,

I saw a little sparrow hopping in the grass today. It made me think of you. Thanks for visiting me.

I Love You and miss you. I wish you were here with me and Mommy. Visit her too.

Love,

Daddy.

Then Mama:

Sophia-

Sorry it took Mommy so long to leave you a note. I miss you every second of every day and wish you were here with us.

I know you are watching over Mommy and Daddy from heaven and please know although you might see us cry you have brought us nothing but happiness.

You are forever our daughter and we will keep your memory with us wherever we go.

I love you so much!

Mommy

Then just a few weeks ago:

Hello little baby. I still miss you. You and your little sisters bring me so much joy. Watch over us Little Birdy.

I'll never leave you angel baby. Please don't ever leave me either.

Love

Daddy

If you want to look, you can go to the site and look. You can see one of the many places Sophia and so many other babies live, go and look. You can post if you want.

The story of the woman who started the site—and now stopped it—is interesting and heartwarming but discouraging in one respect: the thought that some may have tried to take advantage of the loving service she provided for thousands of parents. But she made so many people, including me and Tara, feel so much better about our loss. She made it possible to remember.

Tara and I remembered Sophia with a dove release at the cemetery one year after she died. We heard through our bereavement group about a woman named Macy who did releases. It was a very nice memorial. We played "Somewhere Over the Rainbow," performed by Rufus Wainwright. We spoke a few words.[3] We bought little bottles of bubbles and handed them out. We all blew bubbles together. It was very touching. We had everyone back to our house. It was a strange feeling to be at our house with all of these friends and family and having wine or beer and eating and laughing about whatever. Tara and I had just moved that summer—that would have been August of 2009—so we were showing a lot of people the house for the first time. There was all this going on while we were remembering our little baby—with so many people who were also suffering with child loss.

---

[3] See Appendix B

No doubt, we'd known fears and tears with those people, but it was a party, so to speak. I guess maybe I thought it would be all crying and sharing our pain. But it wasn't. It was fun, to tell the truth. I'm sure Tara and I felt the pain deeply and warmly together that night. And the memorial service was very emotional. But there's joy to think about also. It is, as always, a conflicted sensation, a contradictory experience, when we feel joy at a time purportedly reserved for sadness.

When my brother Brian died, at the funeral, when we all stepped to the casket suspended above the abyss of the grave to toss our carnation onto the coffin, my aunt stepped too close to the gaping maw awaiting my brother's body, slipped on the green faux-grass carpet that covered the mess of dirt mounds left aside from the newly dug pit, and fell knee deep into my brother's eternal bed space, catching herself on her rump at the edge of the hole. An adroit funeral director jumped to her aid and secured her. She was horrified obviously. If she had fallen in—well a shit show at least would have ensued. I asked my parents some time later why they didn't sue. It was embarrassing and scary, and it was the cemetery's fault—they'd not secured and spaced the plot properly—but my parents thought it would just make a bad situation worse. And then the cemetery would just try to blame my aunt and none of it would have been good.

"And for what?" my dad asked me. "For money?"

And I said to myself, "Yes!" Because sometimes people just have to pay. But my parents would never see things that way. And they're probably right.

But anyway, my aunt fell in. Well "fell" really, but "fell in" makes the story so much juicier. And so some hours later we were at repast at my house, and my uncle—my dad's sister's husband, who is always a jokester of sorts—sat down in front of a group of us and laid a napkin across his index and middle fingers of one hand, spread apart palm down, and took the middle and index fingers of his other hand and moved them to replicate walking and said, "Hey look, it's Aunt _______!" as his "finger-legs" fell through the napkin just as my aunt's legs had only a few hours before poked into the devastating real-estate of my brother's eternal rest.

People laughed. I smiled. But my brother was dead.

And I for a long time thought it was insensitive—to me and my deceased brother and to my aunt. But it *was* funny. And a lot of people laughed. In fact, if I remember correctly, I laughed about it when I got into the limousine at the cemetery just a minute or two after it happened, a couple hours *before* my uncle's "re-enactment." It *was* funny. It *is* funny. It's allowed to be, I've learned.

No terror is immune from joy. That first night at the hospital with Tara, waiting for Sophia's stillness to come to us, we had time to laugh. And we thought we were "justly" and "commensurately" corrected with a good dose of humiliating shame the next day. But laughter and joy are unrelenting. I think they insist on triumph.

I recognize, a hundred hundred times now, (and I try to convince myself otherwise a hundred hundred times now) that joy is helping me. And it can sometimes be just a small dose of joy that distills the sea of terror of loss: a little laugh, watching TV or a movie, a good meal, a roller coaster, new "things," and so on.

Yet the checks and balances of terror and joy persist to this day. Sophia is my daughter. I still don't know how to fully incorporate her into my life, but now more than ten years later, I'm leaning towards the "balances": the positive remembrance of Sophia and the positive reflection of that remembrance on the world. At least I'm trying to find the way to do so now. And that's noteworthy for me because there have been times—and *are* times, though fewer and farther between—that I want to go back to Ahab and make the world pay for my pain. But a vague path, or a little deer-run of a way, is appearing for me that Sophia really can make me better. Better than I ever could have been without her.

Sophia's name, written in the sand of some Australian coast.

A Legacy of Toys Never Gifted

In December of 2008, just a few weeks after Sophia slipped away from us...well, Christmas sucked that year, let's just say that. There were lots of egg shells being walked on and lots of feelings and worries and lots of smiles and guilt about those smiles and lots of no smiles and lots of worry about those no smiles and lots of fake smiles and lots of people feeling *really good* about our fake smiles and most of all lots of just wanting the holiday to be over so I could go back into my hole and forget anything other than the pain I was nursing, hiding, keeping in my pocket like contraband.

A year later, for Sophia's one-year memorial, December 2009, we did the dove release, and I felt pretty good about that, but Christmas a few weeks later was particularly difficult.

Here we were, parents expecting to be celebrating our child's first Christmas with no gifts to give—or more accurately, no one to give them to. And of course, now Christmas cards start arriving of young couples with their first child pictured joyfully in red or green and Santa hats. These were people maybe we expected to be young parents with.

Searching for direction, for something good to feel, for something about Sophia we could call "good," Tara and I donated some toys to a local toy drive. I went to Toys R Us and bought some toys—mostly little girl's toys. Tara couldn't come with me. She was on bedrest. She was pregnant with

Charlotte, our first daughter after Sophia. Such a confusing time that was: grieving, pregnant, high risk doctors, check-ups literally every week, bedrest, new home (We couldn't get out of the apartment Sophia was conceived in fast enough—you know, I always thought losing our first baby was the worst because it changed our entire family making experience—it put a sadness and a confusion over even conceiving a child, but now I think about it and when the loss is experienced with siblings, it's so much more difficult to navigate those siblings' emotions and you can't just "up and out" of the accursed place of the tragedy when it is the very home you've already established. Really, I just need to stop putting loss in categories of harder or easier or worse or better. Loss is a loss.) It was a confusing time.

So, I brought the toys to a drop off spot for the toy drive. It was un-celebratory, but I forced myself to feel good and to think of the kids that might enjoy a toy because of me and Tara. Because of Sophia, in fact.

Then, a year later, Charlotte was eleven months old, and Tara and I decided to host what we'd begin calling the Sophia Michelle Toy Drive.

We called up Toys for Tots Foundation and asked if we could host a drop off for a day. They gave us some boxes and stuff: magnets, pens, key chains and so on. We invited family and friends and neighbors to our home. People came with *bags!* Our friends Pat and Sue would come with *bags* of toys! They'd collect from their jobs and from their friends and come with dozens of toys. My Uncle Ed would come with bags of toys from my cousins, his children—all SEVEN of them—a trunk load of toys. We were amazed by people's generosity. And we were proud that this was being done in our baby's memory. It was very nice. And really, I think we all had fun. Again, we realized that we could have good memories in the aftermath of our loss. That somehow, tragedy can transform, somehow.

The next year, somewhat encouraged by the first Sophia Michelle Toy Drive, Tara and I expanded our invites to a broader range of friends, family, and neighbors. Some co-workers of ours attended and neighbors spread the word a bit. We had a face painter and balloon artist come for the kids. I asked some "musically-inclined" students of mine to drop by for Christmas carols. Toys for Tots sent two Marines in their Dress Blues to visit. They spent the whole time at our home. In fact, one sergeant came to our Drive a few years in a row. We got to know him a bit. As it turned out, we brought our babies to the same day care in Uniondale. The last year he came to our event, he told us he was being stationed in Japan and that he would be sad not to attend our Toy Drive again. He was a sweet guy, and I missed seeing him.

Year after year, the number of toys, and the number of visitors grew. We enjoyed having the Drive at our home until it was growing too big. I loved having a collection of toys outside for everyone to see. One time my neighbor had some guys working on his house. An electrician approached me and asked what I was doing. When I explained about Sophia, he nodded his head and said how good it made him feel to see people doing things like this. Then he went to his work van and came back with a fold of bills— A hundred bucks! I told him I couldn't really take cash like that; we weren't really like that. He asked me please that it would make him feel better, that he and his wife had lost a baby and that they never talked about it and he didn't even know that people did things like this. I said thank you and put the cash in an envelope. The next year, I took the envelope from my desk drawer and bought a hundred dollars' worth of toys for the Sophia Michelle Toy Drive, and I remembered that electrician and the baby he and his wife grieved but never talked about.

But the Toy Drive was getting bigger than we could

accommodate. We would annually plan this event and worry about the weather. If it rained, would we be able to accommodate people inside? As a greater number of "strangers" attended, did we *want* anyone inside? Sure, I liked sitting with boxes of toys behind me in front of my firepit in my driveway waving to cars driving by and seeing neighbors coming over smiling with a Toys R Us bag in their arm. But I wanted the Toy Drive to grow.

In 2014, Tara had just given birth in September to Judith, our second child after Sophia, so we ultimately decided that having the Drive at the house, all of the preparing and such, would be too much. We rented a little party room nearby, and the Sophia Michelle Toy Drive moved on.

Now we've had the Toy Drive at a K of C in Seaford for the past few years. We have collected hundreds of toys every year, and every year the total grows. The 2019 Sophia Michelle Toy Drive marked ten years since Sophia died and amassed over five hundred toys. A local newspaper featured our event. Nearly a hundred people came to the drive. Dozens more donated and helped.

From the Sophia Michelle Toy Drive tradition, Tara and I have talked about starting a not for profit—Sophia Michelle Foundation. What a tribute that could be for our little baby. What a way to remember our angel who took flight in her little baby angel wings. To someday announce the Sophia Michelle Foundation? My heart is thumping to just think of it. To have the opportunity to establish a legacy of giving in the name of our little girl, Sophia. I think of all the good Sophia could accomplish: Infant loss awareness, outreach, support, prevention, and scholarships are a few of the ways I have imagined that Sophia could help lives. It's a lot, and it's not easy to do for so many reasons, and maybe it'll never happen, and I have to be ok with that, but the idea that Sophia's memory inspires me to do, *not* to tear down or destroy or withdraw, as maybe I would have liked to at some other time, is the mindset I hope to maintain when I consider my experience as a bereaved parent.

And finishing this book. Publishing it. I've thought of writing a book for my entire life. Truly. When I was a boy, a teen, a young man, always trying to invent some story to write about. My brother Brian encouraged me to read and to write. He told me I could write a book one day. But then he died. And I thought someday I'd write about him. Maybe I will, but it is worth noting that Sophia is the impetus for writing *this*. Writing *now*. I've been writing every day. I've tried to do so several times throughout my life—write every day—but I've never had the discipline. Now I have been writing every day. And I believe it is Sophia that has made me do so. I don't mean it is her death that has made me do so, except, perhaps, in that her death is part of her life, or, rather, part of her present *being*. It is not the *tragedy* of her death that has compelled me to write. Writing this book *has* been therapeutic. It *has* been cathartic. But more than both of those, writing has been *for Sophia*. She has inspired me.

I'm only now beginning to realize the wonder of this phenomenon: Sophia died. In some perspectives, she never *lived*. If that isn't a testament to the power of the human spirit, then I don't know what is. People have run marathons, climbed mountains, changed careers and so on because of the impact of a lost life. In this regard, I don't think anyone would doubt the strength of the human spirit's mighty kingdom. But in this baby? This infant? This fetus? This still child, never born or breathing? *She* has spirit? Well, I know now that she does. I've *felt* it for a long time. I've *wanted* it for a long time. I've *said* it for a long time. But now, feeling the strength to do something I've never done...now I finally *know* it. Sophia's spirit is a living, breathing thing. She surrounds my family. She surrounds all who know her. I have no answers to why she died. I have no belief that "things happen for a reason." All I know is that Sophia is still with us in this way, that this is our daughter, Sophia.

Tara and I with our friend from the marines, Staff Sgt. Bell, at the Sophia Michelle Toy Drive.

Finding a Way

In the week or so that followed Sophia's death, Tara and I spiraled with and around and away and back to each other. But there wasn't anyone else there. Just us in our apartment in Long Beach. On the couch. On the bed. On the floor. On the balcony. Staring out the windows. So often silent. So often crying.

But in this aimless grief, we did have a magnetic force-type attraction for *direction*.

I'm not a Bible reader. I mean, I read the Bible in the same way I might read the Quran or the Bhagavad-Gita or the sutras. They are giant books of otherworldly (and "this-worldly", in fact) wisdom. The Bible is full of tragedy and love, despair and poetry, hubris and humility. It's the simplest truth and the most complex.

In any event, I asked Tara to read some of the Bible with me in that week. We read passages of Job. I'd always known the story of Job but had never actually read it, so I was amazed by how saliently Job conveyed the gloom of grief. I thought of Tara and my own isolation in our apartment when I read, "and no one spoke a word to him, for they saw that his suffering was very great." (2:13).

In my younger life I read the Bible out of a sense of obligation. As I got older, I read for some perceived sense of erudition. But here I was reading Job, with my wife, as we grieved the greatest loss we could have conceived, and I was struck by the sophisticated wisdom, the "spot on" psychology of loss. I guess I had always expected the Bible to be more "primitive." What would a story written 25 centuries or more ago know about loss? In a modern sense or a psychological sense? But here I was, suffering, looking for help, reading, "Yet does not one in a heap of ruins stretch out his hand and in his disaster cry for help?" (30:24) Tara and I would comment as we read or stop and think. In disaster and alone and crying for help. Yes. That's right. That's what we were feeling!

We would read a chapter or two and get tired and close the Bible. In between chapters of Job, Tara and I would say a decade of the rosary together, Tara holding the rosary from her beloved Grandma Mary, and I, the rosary gifted me from my mother when Tara and I were married.

This searching prayerfulness went on throughout the day for a few days.

I can't say I know what reading the Bible or saying the rosary did for us at that time. But now, in retrospect, I think of it like a class in college that you took that you had *no use for* but had you not taken it, you would not be able to have the success you earned professionally. It is a rung on a ladder.

I'm not trying to say that anyone needs to read the Bible for help. All I'm saying is that I knew I needed help. I knew I wasn't going to say Sophia's death would be just a "blip" on the radar of my life. All I'm saying is that I knew I was hurting, and I wanted to feel better. All I'm saying is that the Bible helped me gain some direction. When I read that verse about "stretching out his hand and in his disaster crying for help," I knew that I was going to have to reach out somehow, to get out of Tara and my aimless co-dependency. And I most certainly didn't know this at that time, or I didn't know this in any *cognitive* way, but there were signs and directions and forces pulling or guiding me to *not* push this away or ignore it or abandon Tara. Of course, healing and getting help is a slow arc and I'm certain that I *did* push away and ignore and abandon. But I can't deny the force I felt early on to look for help.

As I've said again and again throughout this remembrance, I don't remember all of the details, but in that week, Tara asked, "What do we do now?"

It was one of those fortunate coincidences, but just as Tara spoke, my mother called. Everyone was walking on eggshells, and I'm sure my mother was nervous just to call our apartment, but she said that my cousin Regina had reached out to her and suggested Tara and I call her. She had lost a child at birth and just wanted to check in.

When I hung up, I reported to Tara what my mother had said.

We wanted to know what to do now. We were stretching out crying for help. So, we called my cousin.

Regina is all parts energy. She's equal parts lion and lamb. She is as quick to laugh as she is to fight. She talked of her pain. She said so many things to Tara and me that we understood and knew. It wasn't like talking to our parents or friends who out of a sense of protectiveness and pain spoke kindly and warmly and gently, with terror at every pause. She spoke in her authoritative way. She was strong and hurt, and she told us what to do. In her very certain, assertive style, Regina told us to "go to a bereavement group."

That may have been the most influential phone call of our grief journey.

Bereavement Group

This is another weird time for which I wish I had a video. I would love to have a video of the time Tara and I spent in the bereavement group at NorthShore/LIJ Hospital. The people we met and suffered with. Ronnie and Teresa. Brian and Kathleen. Dorie and Mike. Danielle and Tommy. Tara and me. All of us heartbroken, stupefied parents. Stretching out our hands, crying out in pain. The babies we came to know. Their brief lives. First Child. Last child. Twins. Died first. Died second. Died in the womb. Died in the crib (an *unthinkable terror!)* Died in the NICU, all tubes and hoses and hope beyond hope, held on with every ounce of infant child spirit and fight and mommy and daddy's LOVE! But all gone.

We shared our stories and fears. We talked week after week about the struggles we had with families and friends and the inability of so many to understand. We talked about our inabilities to understand each other as parents and spouses. We laughed! We had so many laughs. Antics and attitudes and remarks that we found hilarious.

We attended memorial services and benefit walks for each other. We got together for drinks. Went out for meals. Visited each other's homes. We celebrated births and birthdays of "rainbow" babies, as they are commonly called.

While I wish I could better remember all of their stories and all of the things we all said so that I could provide some insight to the great power of the bond we all shared, I will *never* forget those people and what they meant—mean—to me.

One couple, the parents of twins, were attending meetings while their one infant boy was being cared for by the NICU nurses (by the way, some of the greatest people to ever live, in my opinion). His twin brother had just passed away before the bereavement group began. Again -- the parents were attending *bereavement meetings* as their other child was *struggling to live in the NICU*! They were coping and healing and suffering at the SAME TIME!

It was a devastation of hope that their child fought like a baby warrior but sadly lost his battle. And his death was felt by all of us. So, we went to the funeral to show our support. And I never felt like I belonged at a funeral as much as I did then.

What we went through together is mind boggling.

I think I really relied on those bonds to have a "safe" environment to cope. It was fabricated of course—even artificial, in some respects: we only knew each other for this one reason. But a broken bone needs a cast, and as such, the bereavement group gave me and Tara, and I would imagine the others in our group, the structure and support to heal.

At the center of that structure and support was Ivy Diamond.

Our bereavement group has drifted apart, as it should, and that confused me at first. I thought that maybe I was being abandoned again, and I felt really uncomfortable interacting socially outside of that group. But again, the group was the cast. Sure when the cast comes off, the limb feels weak and naked and vulnerable. But off it must come. We drifted apart. I still see them on Facebook now and then. Their lives have grown and moved in all the ways one would expect. And I think of them often. We drifted apart.

But I have stayed in touch somewhat with Ivy.

It's difficult to explain how a person can so impact a life when I hardly know the person. We did not know Ivy for years. We didn't spend much personal time with her. We saw her over the course of a few months. We met for a couple of hours. She facilitated discussion. She avoided, for the most part, talking about herself and her infant loss. We knew of her loss and at times she shared, but she made it clear that our stories were of greater importance.

Maybe that's it. Maybe when someone puts others before herself, maybe that's when you really get to know her. Not so unlike a hero who saves someone in a building fire or a car wreck. The hero is merely a shadow of a face in the life of the victim. Literally *nothing* does the imperiled one know of the rescuer. But that relationship has changed *both* their lives forever.

The selflessness is all I needed to know about Ivy. She's a good person who helped us. We were all in the burning building. We were all in the wreck. She was the hero who jeopardized her own life, re-lived her sadness and loss every time she met with us, told her own family "no" for a few hours a week to help families she didn't know.

Ivy Diamond is a hero.

In 2016 or so, Ivy emailed me. I hadn't seen her in years. She was looking for someone to share a story of loss and healing for her annual bereavement conference at NorthShore/LIJ, I was so thrilled to hear from her, but more importantly, I was joyful to contribute in this way, to help her help others. I thought that maybe some of the goodness Ivy did, I could do too.

But most important, I started thinking of giving a talk like this as not "mine" but Sophia's.

After the talk that October, Martha Weiss of St. Kilian's

GAPS program asked if I could present a similar talk at her own annual prayer service.[4]

It was after these occasions that I first seriously considered the idea that I was healing, that Sophia was having a different role in my life. I felt as though maybe I was moving from loss to gain, regarding Sophia.

It was an uncomfortable realization. In what crazy way could that poor little baby's death be a good thing? But that's it: I had considered Sophia's *death* as the "be all." I think that presenting those talks, first for Ivy and then for Martha, channeled my thoughts towards Sophia's "life": what she was —and *is*—to us. The potential for help or even *joy* to result from Sophia assured me that I had been considering Sophia in a narrow lens for too long a time.

In the end, that's what bereavement groups do. What people like Ivy Diamond do. They widen the lens through which we can consider our loss. Some people give a narrow lens. Drugs and alcohol can be a lens. Some people think they're giving you *the* lens: the *only way* to see. Ivy didn't give me *the* lens, but *a* lens. Perhaps a lens that simply helped me to know that there are lenses at all with which we can view tragedy in a better way.

---

[4] See Appendix C

Today is the Best Day of My Life

I have learned—or I am learning—in these last couple of years, that my language can very much define my reality. This has been a struggle for me at times to accept because I can say anything I want, but saying of the thing doesn't make it true. If it's pouring out and I say it's a sunny day, that's not defining my reality, that's lying to myself. However, if it's raining out and I say it's a beautiful day, then that's a different story. That's subjective. Who's to say the rain isn't beautiful? What I've realized is that quite a bit of my feeling lost in my life, quite a bit of my sadness may have been a matter of perspective.

I can't really say why I've felt this way. Maybe a childhood trauma. Maybe some breach of trust, however minor or major, has warped my ability to gauge the goodness of my life. Maybe it was just "me." But the fact is that I would say I didn't have a very happy childhood. Or maybe the fact is better stated: I don't remember seeing joy in my childhood.

I had everything a child could want to be happy, but I was plagued, for as long as I can remember, with a sense of sadness. (I'm certain this is a pretty clinical definition of depression, which absolutely runs in my family).

When I was a boy, maybe ten or eleven, I was sulking around the house at some family party of one sort or another. My uncle Daniel stopped me in the kitchen and asked me why

I wasn't smiling. I don't remember what I said, but Uncle Daniel told me, "Walk around the house once and smile when you come back to the kitchen."

So, I walked a "lap" around the house, from the kitchen to the living room to the dining room and back to him in the kitchen and he was standing there smiling and I did everything I could to show him I wasn't having it. I grilled him hard!

So, Uncle Daniel shook his head and said do it again.

After four or five times, I couldn't help bursting out in laughter. He smiled as he held me by the arm and looked at me and said, "That's the smile factory, Michael. You can walk through it anytime you want. Just remember that smiles are *made*. Okay?"

I said okay as I tried unsuccessfully to shed the silly smile my uncle's loving tease produced.

Then Uncle Daniel said, "Michael, today is the best day of your life."

Suddenly, I grew serious again and responded emphatically that it wasn't.

Yes, it is, he said to me simply. But I pointed out that today is miserable, and yesterday was better.

He said no, that yesterday is never better than today.

So, I pointed out that tomorrow might be better than today.

He said no, that tomorrow is never better than today.

I said what if today is the *worst* day of my life.

He said no, that today is always the best day of your life. That today is the best day because we *have it*. For as long as we have *today* it is the best day of your life.

I guess I understood what he meant at the time, but I have understood what he meant better as an adult, even though at times I have failed to understand, or I have simply rejected what he meant.

And I am realizing now, I think, what he really meant, and I'm wondering how far I can push his philosophy.

The day my brother left and disappeared, that was the best day of my life.

The day I married Tara, that was the best day of my life.

The day I learned my brother Brian was dead, that was the best day of my life.

The day Charlotte was born, that was the best day of my life.

The day we took Judith home from the NICU, that was the best day of my life.

The day we learned Sophia was conceived, that was the best day of my life.

The day Sophia died, that was the best day of my life.

Those each were the best days of my life because I had them.

Today is the best day of my life. Because I have it.

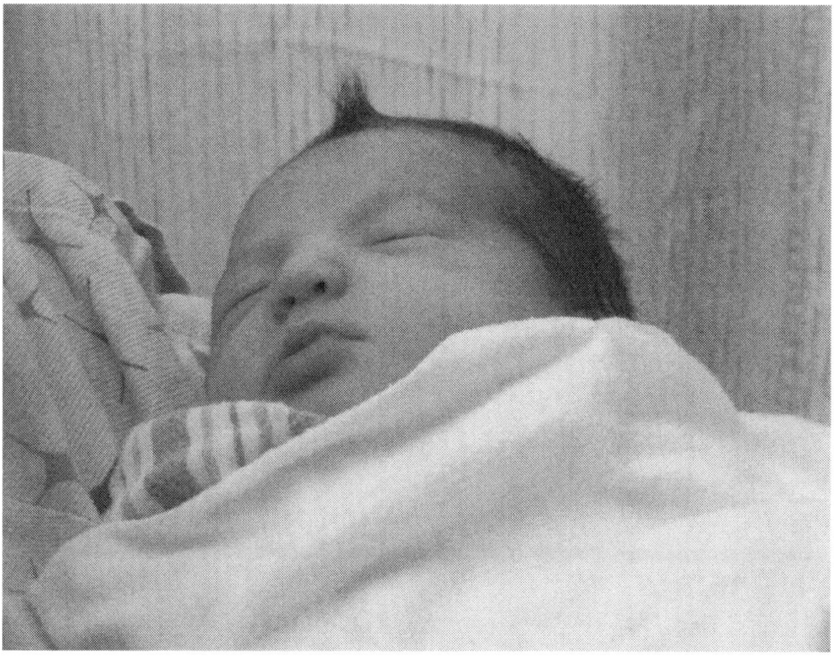

Newborn Charlotte

Judith home from the NICU

Brian

I have on a few occasions throughout this writing referred to my brother Brian.

Brian, my brother, seven years older than I, the second of six children, the second of four boys and two girls, took his own life on September 21, 1993. He was twenty-four. I was seventeen, beginning my senior year in high school. He stepped in front of an oncoming train some hundreds of yards west of Lynbrook train station. He was found the next day in the railroad's late summer overgrowth.

While this book is about Sophia, I had plans to devote some substantial space to Brian in this book. There was going to be great tearing of hair and gnashing of teeth. I had driven myself to tears just thinking of the climax his part in this book would be.

But my plan—my mind—has changed as I've written this.

This change in direction is not a reflection of any change in my actual experience of my older brother, but instead a change in focus. Maybe there will be a time for the gnashing of teeth and so on, but right now, there's only one image of him I want to see: a picture of him playing guitar or piano, or painting, or of a blizzard in the late seventies when I was just a toddler and he stood beside me as the protector I always thought him to be, or when he was maybe seventeen or eighteen and shirtless and his physique to me then was so impressive, or maybe as a boy in his "army" helmet or in his CYO basketball t-shirt from Saint Benny's, back in Queens.

Images like these, hundreds and hundreds of them in photographs and in my mind were eclipsed by a very different and sad picture of him.

That sad picture had usurped my love and joy of Brian for a long, long time. But it's possible that I've been thinking of Brian the wrong way all these years. No, I guess that's not fair. I've been grieving. I guess I can't say that it's been "the wrong way." But I'm wondering if I'm getting to a better place in my grief. And, as I have with my baby Sophia, I want to reorient myself. It's possible that my thoughts of Sophia, of the good she has been in my life, have transformed my thoughts about Brian.

So, Brian, a word please...

Brian,

I wish I could have said goodbye. I'm not angry at you. I can't ever understand what your thoughts were. We tried, Brian, to show you the love we thought could save you.

Brian, for twenty-five years I have wondered where you are. And I have looked for you. I have literally looked for you. I have fantasized that you weren't really dead and that I would see you on the street or in a homeless shelter or a psych ward somewhere, that I might stop at a light and look to see the driver beside me was you. I have fantasized that you might one day walk through the front door of Mom and Dad's house in Lynbrook and we'd all be there and you'd just look at us and say sorry and cry and we would all hug you and say everything's ok now, Brian, don't be sorry.

But I know where you are now. Or I'm starting to know.

I wish so many things. But those wishes sometimes confuse me. Sometimes they spin me around, and maybe I lose track of myself.

So, all I can do right now is say thank you. Thank you, big brother, for telling me that day so long ago and all those days after that to read and to read and to read. Thank you for showing me what to read. Thank you for telling me to write. Thank you for reading those silly stories I wrote (and I wrote them all for you—for you to read, and nobody else has seen any of those and I've destroyed all of that long ago and I regret doing that) and telling me they were good and not calling me out for copying S.E. Hinton or Tolkien or Hemingway or Steinbeck or whomever I may have been reading at that particular age. Thank you for telling me about the classes you took and the authors you read and the philosophy you learned. And when I told you I didn't understand it, thanks for telling me that understanding didn't matter, that I just had to read it.

Thanks for writing letters to me when you went to college. I never wrote letters to anyone else. I wrote Deirdre when she went to Thailand, but I was a man by then, and I was just a kid when we wrote to each other when you were at school. I wish I'd saved those letters.

At school one day, when, while I was writing to you, a classmate asked me what I was doing, I said, "Writing a letter to my brother. He's away at school."

"Why don't you just call him?"

He didn't understand. So many people didn't understand.

So, I can only thank you for everything you were and are to me, for everything that made us laugh and everything that went wrong.

Goodbye, Brian.

Love always,

Michael

My Brother, Brian

"Where are You?"

"Where are you, Sophia?"

"I'm here, Daddy. I'm in Mommy's love for you. In Charlotte's and Judith's love for you. I'm in Charlotte's hair and Judith's nose. Daddy, I'm here in your eyes and in Mommy's lips. I'm here with you when you cry and laugh. I'm here with you when you get angry or feel lost. I'm here in this book, Daddy. I'm in your voice. I'm here in the breeze and the sunshine. I'm in the rain, Daddy. And in the blizzards too, Daddy. I'm in the leaky roof and the weedy lawn and the shoveling of the snow and the traffic jams and fender benders. Daddy, I'm in that hug you give to Mommy, or when you hold hands, I'm here. I'm here when Judith cries out in the night. I'm here when Judith snuggles on your lap. I'm here in Charlotte's kindness for others, in her gentle love for others.

"I'm here, Daddy! I'm right *here*! Can't you see me?"

“Here I Am”

“Where are you, Daddy?”

“I’m here, Sophia. I’m right here.”

“Can you see me, Daddy?”

“I can see you now, Sophia. I didn’t know where I was. I was lost, Little Birdy. I’m sorry. ”

“I know, Daddy. I love you.”

“I love you too, Little Baby. Good night.”

“Good night, Daddy.”

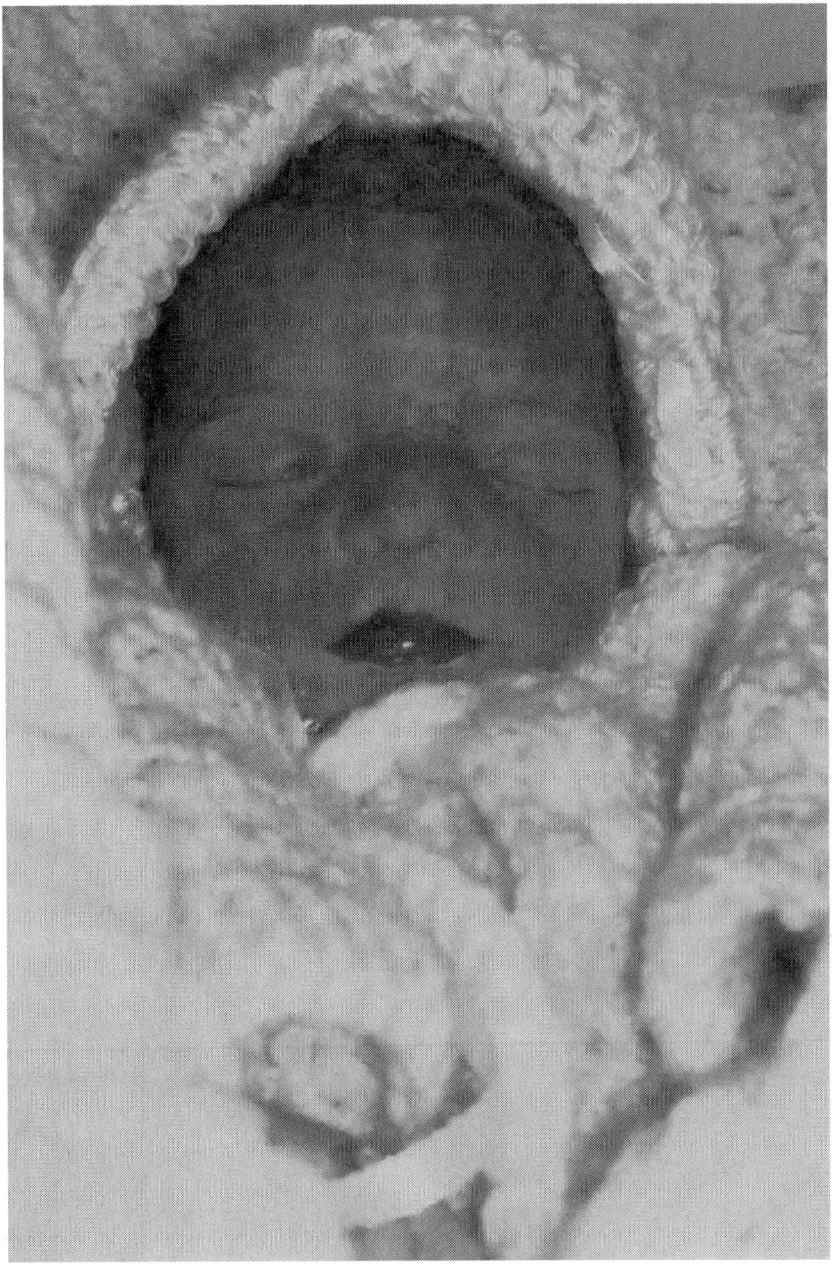

Our Baby, Sophia

Epilogue

I

Writing about loss and sadness is so difficult because the terrain is always shifting.

We, as humans, do everything we can to put the trek in straight lines, though it's anything but straight. For example, the stages of grief: denial, anger, bargaining, depression, and acceptance. Very linear looking. I can manage that, right? Like a roadmap journey through grief: head straight on Denial, then travel south to Anger, at the McDonald's take a left on Bargaining, then drive for a while on Depression until you can take a left and head north to Acceptance.

But it isn't like that at all. And it's not like anyone (anyone serious anyway) really says that it is that way. It's just we see those five daunting, but very relatable words, and we see them in order and we say okay, I can get there. But, in my experience, the fact of the matter has been "getting there," (or here, or over there, or there again, and now back here) is an event that occurs over and over again.

I never moved "through" grief like a tunnel, per se. It's a timeless and orderless ordeal. While I'd like to claim that at the finish of this book I have accepted my loss(es) and sadness and that I have completed my grief journey, a more accurate statement might be that at the time of the finish of this book, I am experiencing "acceptance." For the time being. Right now. For now, anyway. I might be angry at dinner time. I might deny before I go to bed. I might be depressed for the winter. And then accepting again next spring before it starts all over again.

You'd have to read from people more informed than I am, but grief might very well last a lifetime. I am hoping that a set of thoughts and behaviors I am trying to adopt might affect a greater duration of acceptance, but the anger and depression and bargaining and denial—the sadness generally—might come and go.

The real challenge, I think, is ignoring the popular-type notion that grief is something to be "gotten over." As if the hoped-for acceptance will make a clean sheet on which we can write the rest of our happy lives as though the sadness never came. Now again, *nobody* who has studied grief—that I've read or heard of—thinks such an outcome is possible, or even desirable. Again, this is a "popular" notion of grief because grief can be such an interrupter of work and relationships and fun. And of course, it's painful. We want "it" to be over sooner than later. For ourselves and for others.

And yes, it is good for the sadness to diminish. It is good to get back to work. We don't want relationships to end because of our sadness. Of course not. And the sadness *can* end.

But the "grief" might last forever. The shifting directions of our emotional lives might always be the reality we have to live with.

That is the hard part. That we as a culture are unwilling so often to accept that grief can change us. That we as a culture are unwilling to accept death as a factor that evinces change *here* for the *living*. That we as a culture are unwilling to allow the bereaved to honor and remember and experience their loss in a litany of complicated ways. And that can be confusing for the rest of the world, watching and waiting for the mourners to get through those five stages and return things to the way they were before death descended and took away all of that joy.

But there is a way back for us. I don't know what it is. Only in retrospect can I speak of how I may have come to terms with my loss, but I don't think I could've predicted then what I'm experiencing now. But there is some advice. And it's not mine; it was given to me. To Tara and me, actually. Sometime after Sophia died, Tara and I went to see a child loss counselor, Nancy Berlow. We asked her how do we know if we're dealing with our loss in a healthy way. She reminded us to avoid drugs and alcohol. She reminded us to talk about our loss and feelings, with each other and with others. Generally, she said move toward productive activities and avoid destructive ones.

Simple, right?

I know that it's not, but my hope, and I include myself in this prescription, is that we can be more patient and understand that loss comes in many different ways. If we can listen to each other's stories, we might be more inclined to respect and love one another. And in that case, we can have more space in our lives for spiritual and emotional wellness. And that goes for all of us. Literally everyone. Because I think we're all in need of healing.

Not everyone has suffered the pain of loss in a literal "end of life" way. But that doesn't mean we don't experience that same sensation of grief, perhaps for some undetected loss. I myself have struggled with a lifetime of "grief," of sadness, of loss, of depression—long before I knew death. I can't say I know why.

But maybe the advice for the bereaved is the same for the "aggrieved." Talk. Avoid drugs and alcohol. Be productive, not destructive.

I know it's more complicated than that. But in the end, I think our sadnesses can be transformed if our stories can *just be heard!*

II

There are many who suffer loss and don't have the experience Tara and I have. I'm sure different people's predispositions toward emotional life and pain produce different responses to loss or suffering. There are people who experience loss and experience the pain and the tears but within a reasonably short span of time are back and active and laughing and smiling.

Why?

I used to think it was because those people didn't love like I could. Fully and with "reckless abandon," as the expression goes. I used to feel that those people who didn't "feel the hurt" were denying their emotions.

Clearly, that's a misguided notion.

There are stories of Holocaust survivors who go on to lead productive and joyous lives because of the chance they were given, just as there are stories of Holocaust survivors who go on to lead destructive lives because of the pain they were given. Similar accounts can be culled from the stories of survivors of a multitude of destructions and traumas. The same events occur to a group of people, but the outcomes are starkly different.

Why?

The truth is that some people's ability to cope "better" or more quickly might be "built-in" long before the opportunity for loss is experienced. Many social and genetic theorists suggest that "sadness" might be either socially or genetically determined, so that it comes to us much like a standout athlete or intellect might seem to possess the benefits of good fortune on the field or in academia "naturally." But was that ability learned socially or delivered genetically.

But -- in either case -- it doesn't have to mean I'm any more doomed to sadness than the meek are doomed to frailty. Again and again, we hear stories of the hard-working hustler who makes the team or the study-a-holic who gets straight A's in spite of "physical or intellectual limitations."

I think I'd like to consider myself in the "emotional" context of this category. I have been, it seems, predisposed to sadness, perhaps, for some social or genetic factors. But I am, so to speak, working out and studying as much as I can in order to "learn" how to choose joy. I just envision myself walking around my old kitchen as my uncle Daniel instructed, "through the smile factory."

Losing our little baby was crushing. But we said we would get through it together. Before we ever conceived a child or spent a night together as husband and wife, we said we would get through it together. And, besides, I don't know how to do it alone. I need so many of the people in my life in order to successfully "get through it." I need Tara, more than anyone, in so many ways. And that can sometimes be an unfair burden on a spouse, a lover, a friend, a partner, a burden unexpected when attempting to survive the grief cycle.

I still have a ton of work to do. And, as I now know, the work may never "end."

But that's not a bad thing. We work a lifetime as a parent or a friend or a lover. We work a lifetime as a homeowner or an angler, a gearhead or an artist. We work for the things we love.

Maybe that's it. We work for what we love. We don't bemoan such work. When we suffer loss and pain, can we fall out of love with ourselves? Do we fail to see the value of "working" towards our relationships, our hearts, our *selves*?

Maybe.

Maybe for one of the first times in my life, I need to stop right now and think, "I want to live. I want to smile. I want to make others smile."

Maybe for the first time in my life, I need to stop right now and think, "I love myself." And I need to work.

III

It occurs to me that everything I'm saying might be "bullshit". Dull, sentimental musings. Self-serving drivel. God, I hope not, but I see that it might be perceived that way.

All I can hope it that as cliché as my thoughts probably are, they are—more than my thoughts—my feelings and my experiences. They are real. And it has been very painful sometimes to be myself. If I'm learning now that the pain has really been *fighting* myself, fighting *knowledge* of myself, well, then that's a liberating epiphany. But no matter what, losing my little girl was awful. I wish she were here with us. For my sake. For Tara's sake. For my daughters' sakes.

No matter what rhetorical gymnastics I pull off, the fact will always remain that Tara and I lost a love of our lives. And no matter how cliché my thoughts might be, the loss is deep and real, our pain is deep and real. My thoughts are real. The fact will remain that depression and anxiety are very much a part of my life, and the pain is real. My thoughts are real.

For so long, so many people like me are afraid to tell our stories, our feelings, because we're afraid of being invalidated. We're afraid of being vulnerable—or of articulating our vulnerability. We're afraid of appearing weak. We're afraid of being judged weak or incompetent.

The fact of the matter is, in my observation, that if sadness and loss and anxiety are *weak,* then a hell of a lot of us are really, really weak and maybe we should get off of each others' cases about it. How are we *helping* each other, for Pete's sake? Are we even trying? Or do we try harder to simply get others to be like us, to think and feel like us?

Stories are a lot like maps. They can show us the way. Maps show us the way to go and stories can show us the way to live by showing us how others live. That's what stories do. Or can do. If we're open to them.

Appendix A

This is the speech I wrote for Ivy Diamond's Memorial Service at North Shore/LIJ

Good afternoon and thank you so much for having me today and for hearing me.

Over the summer my sister sent me an article about grief. The article expressed very thoughtfully that there is no shame in grief. That grief can be something we OWN. Proudly. In all of its frustrating and tearful forms, grief is a critical part of healing. Expressing our fears, and concerns, and guilts and angers and sadnesses—THAT is healing.

But I just want to say that I'm just a guy. Just a dad. A husband. I am NOT an expert on grief or loss. I'm not a therapist. I took Psych 101 at Queens College about 20 years ago and that was about that. So anything I say today I say from SHARED EXPERIENCE. It doesn't give me any authority. I don't mean to say that my experience of trying to heal is the way to do it. It's just the way I've thought about it and maybe if you're feeling lost—maybe it can help.

But before I talk about healing, it's important that I talk about being injured about being wounded...our daughter's name is Sophia Michelle Flood. She was born on December 5, 2008. She was born still. I still can't understand it really. On December 4 my wife, Tara, didn't feel the baby moving. She called the doctor and was told to go to the hospital. I left my work to pick Tara up at hers and take her to the hospital. The ultrasound was silent. That rhythmic thumping we all LOVED to hear at regular visits was gone. The nurse said, "I'm sorry. I don't hear anything. The baby's gone." Tara cried a cry that only a mother who's lost a child can cry. I still hear it in my mind. It was a howl, really. And I turned immediately to rage, as I usually did, cursing the doctor and nurses that were present — cursing them for their incompetence. I still regret that. Not for their sake, but for Tara's — that my first reaction was to misplace anger rather than deliver comfort and compassion to my wife. I feel guilty about that.

When Tara's OB came in, we asked her why did this happen? She shrugged — not callously but confused and saddened. She said, "I don't know. These things happen."

On the afternoon of December 5th, more than 24 hours after that silent ultrasound, after hours of labor, Tara delivered Sophia. She was two and a half pounds. The nurses put a cap and sweater on our baby. We received her in our hands. I held her little body as Tara undressed her. I don't know why we did that. She needed to be real? We needed to see her body? I don't know. She was cool to the touch but peaceful. We cried. We asked a priest to come and baptize her.

And the next day — we went home. When I went to get the car from the valet, this kid must've seen some maternity something or other on my receipt — he got out of the car and said, "Congratulations man." I put my hand up to him and said quietly, "The baby died, please don't say anything to my wife." How many times in the coming weeks did loose acquaintances or neighbors see us and ask, "Oh how's the baby?" And we would look away with some crazy sense of embarrassment and say, "Oh it didn't work out" or "We lost the baby" or just shake our heads — like another little death every time that happened.

I will tell you though, that there is a certain fondness with which I remember those weeks after Sophia's death. Specifically, the closeness between me and Tara. Like the world was against us and we alone could protect each other. But then we go back to work. Or we get to the dry cleaners or shopping finally. Or we go out with some friends for dinner and everybody says, "Oh they're better. Good."

And then we get into our first argument about who should've emptied the dishwasher or something stupid like that, and the protection we offered each other over the preceding weeks or months had evaporated — we fell completely "into ourselves." Completely isolated. Fears, guilts, sadnesses, expectations, emotional pains, and needs of all kinds went without being spoken about or tended to.

THEN is when the damage really began.

It is from THAT time that we need healing. That isolation.

I just heard the other day somebody compare parents who have lost a child to two burn victims trying to hug each other. Perfect analogy. Even comforting each other became painful.

But that isolation is a reflex. Just like flinching or blinking, it's a protective measure. Those of us who have suffered in this way curl into ourselves when our little angels leave us because we brace ourselves for IMPACT. We brace ourselves for the crushing blow of loss and all of its "attendant" demons: Sleeplessness, nightmares, paralyzing anxiety, lingering or "inexplicable" sadness — in other words depression — bouts of rage, substance abuse, feelings of guilt or shame, disconnectedness, paranoia... and the happy list goes on: each symptom of our sadness an obstacle to healthy relationships and healing.

So...that's the pain. That's the injury we all have suffered.

Sophia is our first-born daughter. She is buried at St. Charles Cemetery. We went to her grave EVERY week for years. Flowers, stuffed animals, balloons, floral arrangements that looked like birthday cakes, holiday themed or seasonal themed decorations, sobbing, cleaning the stone, talking to Sophia, talking to ourselves...Only when the schedule of two children made it too difficult to get over there every week did we stop.

Sophia has two little sisters now — both of whom outlived Sophia the minute they were born: Charlotte nearly 7 and Judith 2 years old.

I mention Charlotte and Judith because — I DON'T KNOW if they are part of my healing. They are my joy every day — but not necessarily my healing. I mean, what kind of pressure would that be to put on two little girls anyway? Though I think that I expected possibly their births to mitigate somehow my sense of loss, in retrospect, I realize that that was always impossible.

In fact, I resented when people — friends and acquaintances mostly, said, "Just get pregnant again." A friend of mine said, "Just knock her up again. You'll be ok." I mean this was like DAYS after we lost our little girl. I mean, we're supposed to just "get prego again" and forget the fact that I held a lifeless child??? No way. Not that easy.

In any case, our healing — my wife and mine — may have begun almost immediately without our realizing...my cousin, who experienced a stillbirth — encouraged us to participate in a bereavement group. So, we did.

So Like zombies we just walked in. If somebody had told us to walk into a burning building, we would have done so as easily. There was no understanding of healing. It was a stunned reflex.

But we met Ivy Diamond. As many of you have also. So possibly without YOUR realizing — meeting Ivy, participating in a bereavement group, being HERE today — you're healing.

Sadly, most people don't understand the loss we have experienced. And that is one of the biggest obstacles to our healing. That's the <u>gift</u> of the bereavement groups, but that ignorance on most people's parts prevents the one thing that CAN initiate our healing — talking about it, communication. When no one understands, we feel silly talking about our loss.

You know, I believe in signs, and so did many of the people we were in the bereavement group with. I remember our friend Brian, whose son Liam died. Brian worked in a bank, and his office was having a promotion or something, so they had these pins made up that said "Talk to me about L.I.A.M." Liam. It was like Life Insurance and Mortgages or something, but the pin said TALK TO ME ABOUT LIAM...When Brian showed us the pin at a meeting, I think we all cheered! Like YES that's RIGHT talk to me about my KID! It was a victory.

So, after a short while — weeks or so — Tara and I went to talk with a grief counselor. We asked her, "How do we know we're being healthy? How do we know we're handling this the right way?" She assured us we were. Avoid destructive behavior and TALK about your feelings, your loss — to each other, to others...anyone — Sophia's your child. TALK about her.

So, we did. Let me tell you I think I made A LOT of people REALLY uncomfortable. But she is my daughter. So, I talked about her.

But in the end, that only goes so far. Sadly, the people that know of your loss in many cases become tired of hearing about it. Many people think: "It's time to get over it."

So, we hold on to our loss, and our healing is interrupted. Bitterness. Self—centeredness. A dark hole of thoughts that belong ONLY TO ***ME.***

How many of us struggle to be happy for friends and loved ones who become pregnant or who have successful pregnancies? That is a toxic bitterness. It poisoned me. And Tara. And still does in many respects.

It's not a feeling I enjoy. I love kids! I love when people are pregnant! I wanted that joy back.

But how?

Healing is hard work. It doesn't just happen. Physical Therapy can take months. Psychotherapy can take years. Grief can take YEARS — of hard work. Thoughtful commitment to feeling better.

Some time after Sophia died, my sister's friend's dad died. I don't know why, but I HAD to go to her father's wake. That wake and my small condolences gave me one of my first opportunities to GET OUT OF MYSELF.

Now — years later, I have adopted that as my mantra for healing — GET OUT OF MYSELF.

We lost Sophia on December 5. A year later we planned a little memorial. Family and close friends met us at the cemetery for a few words and a dove release.

But that one-year memorial was a particularly difficult time. Tara and I were so upset because by December 2009 we expected to be celebrating baby's first Christmas. Instead we were remembering her death.

We decided to buy toys and donate them to a local toy drive in Sophia's name. I think I figured if we weren't going to buy toys for <u>our</u> child, maybe we could buy them for someone else's. It was <u>not</u> easy to do. There was a certain amount of bitterness as I dropped the toys in the bin. Tara couldn't even come with me. I certainly didn't feel like we were healing.

Then the next year we donated a small sum of money to Toy's For Tots Foundation, again in Sophia's name.

And now, for the last several years Tara and I have hosted an annual Toys For Tots toy drive. We've collected hundreds of toys and remember Sophia each time.

Last spring Tara and I heard about the Star Legacy foundation. We participated in their walk to raise awareness for Stillbirths. Many of you have possibly heard of it already. They are doing things like fundraising for research and awareness and comfort and lobbying state governments to provide birth certificates for stillborns. I know that's something I'd love to have for Sophia.

But I sometimes wish I could just tell someone where it hurts, though. You know, "It hurts right here. In my heart." I want someone to take the pain away. I want to go to my doctor and say, "It hurts right here, take it out!" But I know it doesn't work that way.

Though I wish to wear my pain like a badge of honor, my pain is no worse than anyone else's. Though I want the world to stop because I HELD MY LIFELESS DAUGHTER, I know that it doesn't work that way.

I just want to share with you that healing might not ever be a process I expect to end. I might always have that pain. But if I can transform — even if it's a constant battle to do so — if I can transform that pain into a joy of helping others in Sophia's name — that's a pain I can accept — for her.

I want to remember Sophia gently and lovingly. Her 28 weeks in mommy's belly. The first time I heard her heartbeat. The first time I saw her grainy picture on an ultrasound. The first clothes and stuffed animals Tara bought for her. The time I went to Kathleen of Donegal's in Rockville Centre to buy little Irish onesies for her. The first time I felt her kick. The first — and only — time I held her. I will always be proud of the time I had with her.

Sophia can make others happier through me. I want to get out of myself and use my loss, use Sophia to make an impression on the world. A positive impression. I can get a tattoo of her name on my arm. I can have her name engraved in a brick or a bracelet on my wrist. I can light a candle in her name. I can have a Mass or service said for her. All of these are things we've done. All of us have done these things — and they help — in their own ways.

But to me, I want my memory to be even bigger than that. I want Sophia to affect the world through me. It might be volunteering at a soup kitchen, visiting a senior home, supporting the special Olympics, donating time to a place of worship. Maybe it's taking your partner out to dinner and holding hands and saying I'm thinking of you. I'm here for you.....I don't know what it might be. Because I'm still not there myself. But I'm working on it.

I just want you all to know that I consider you my friends now. We're in a fraternity of suffering — or maybe it's a fraternity of healing. In either case, you're friends of mine now. And your angels and my angel are now up in heaven giggling and playing together. I don't know if you believe in heaven. It doesn't matter. I know Sophia's in a place. I know it. It's a place where the carpet is made of clouds and stars float in front of the children's faces like lightning bugs and the sun says good morning and the crescent moon wears a nightcap — if your loss is recent, I know my daughter, and she is up there right now welcoming your little baby. And if your loss is old, Sophia is jumping rope or blowing bubbles with a giant bubble wand. That's what she does now. I know it.

Thank you — everyone — thank you for giving me a chance to heal today.

Appendix B

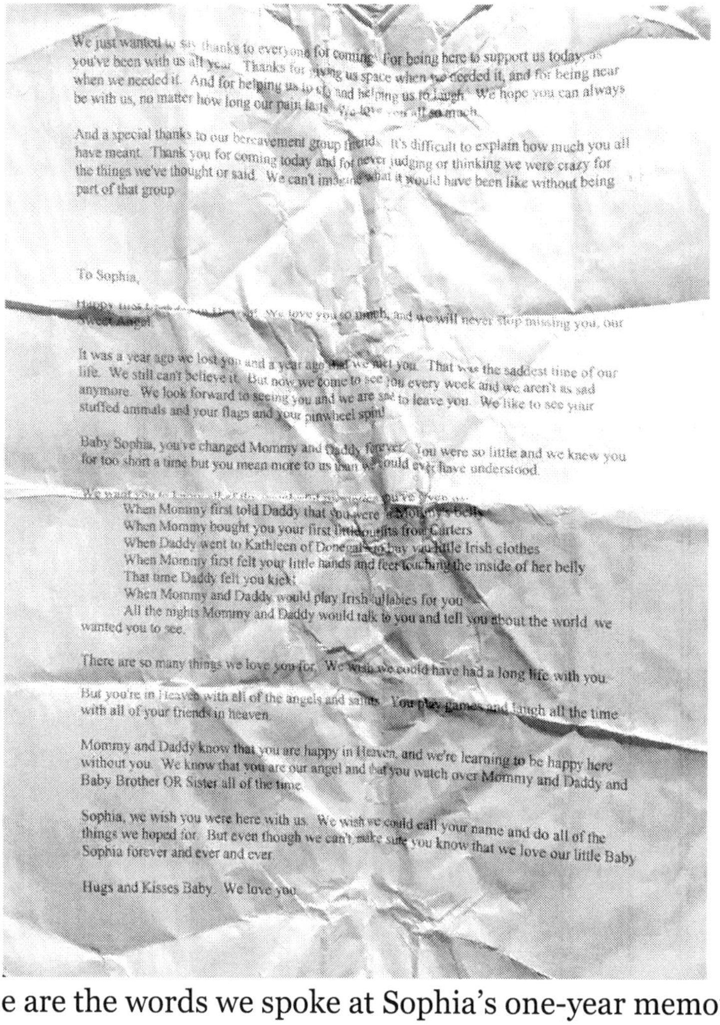

We just wanted to say thanks to everyone for coming. For being here to support us today, as you've been with us all year. Thanks for giving us space when we needed it, and for being near when we needed it. And for helping us to cry and helping us to laugh. We hope you can always be with us, no matter how long our pain lasts. We love you all so much.

And a special thanks to our bereavement group friends. It's difficult to explain how much you all have meant. Thank you for coming today and for never judging or thinking we were crazy for the things we've thought or said. We can't imagine what it would have been like without being part of that group.

To Sophia,

Happy [illegible] in Heaven. We love you so much, and we will never stop missing you, our Sweet Angel.

It was a year ago we lost you and a year ago that we met you. That was the saddest time of our life. We still can't believe it. But now we come to see you every week and we aren't as sad anymore. We look forward to seeing you and we are sad to leave you. We like to see your stuffed animals and your flags and your pinwheel spin!

Baby Sophia, you've changed Mommy and Daddy forever. You were so little and we knew you for too short a time but you mean more to us than we would ever have understood.

We want you to know [illegible] you've been ...

When Mommy first told Daddy that you were in Mommy's belly
When Mommy bought you your first little outfits from Carters
When Daddy went to Kathleen of Donegal to buy you little Irish clothes
When Mommy first felt your little hands and feet touching the inside of her belly
That time Daddy felt you kick!
When Mommy and Daddy would play Irish lullabies for you
All the nights Mommy and Daddy would talk to you and tell you about the world we wanted you to see.

There are so many things we love you for. We wish we could have had a long life with you.

But you're in Heaven with all of the angels and saints. You play games and laugh all the time with all of your friends in heaven.

Mommy and Daddy know that you are happy in Heaven, and we're learning to be happy here without you. We know that you are our angel and that you watch over Mommy and Daddy and Baby Brother OR Sister all of the time.

Sophia, we wish you were here with us. We wish we could call your name and do all of the things we hoped for. But even though we can't, make sure you know that we love our little Baby Sophia forever and ever and ever.

Hugs and Kisses Baby. We love you.

These are the words we spoke at Sophia's one-year memorial.

The paper copy is creased and wrinkled from opening-closing-and-reopening and lives in the box we keep upon our bedroom dresser, along with the sad few things that once were Sophia's.

"We just wanted to say thanks to everyone for coming. For being here to support us today, as you've been with us all year. Thanks for giving us space when we needed it, and for being near when we needed it. And for helping us to cray and helping us to laugh. We hope you can always be with us, not matter how long our pain lasts. We love you all so much.

And a special thanks to our bereavement group friends. It's difficult to explain how much you all have meant. Thank you for coming today and for never judging or thinking we were crazy for the things we've thought or said. We can't imagine what it would have been like without being part of that group.

To Sophia, Happy first Birthday in Heaven! We love you so much and we will never stop missing you, our Sweet Angel. It was a year ago we lost you and a year ago we met you. That was the saddest time of our life. We still can't believe it. But now come to see you every week, and we aren't as sad anymore. We look forward to seeing you and we are sad to leave you. We like to see our stuffed animals and your flags and your pinwheel spin!

We want you to know all of the wonderful memories you've given us: When Mommy first told Daddy you were in Mommy's belly. When Mommy bought you your first little outfits from Carters. When Daddy went to Kathleen's of Donegal to buy little Irish clothes. When Mommy first felt your little hands and feet touching the inside of her belly. That time Daddy felt you kick! When Mommy and Daddy would play Irish lullabies for you. All the nights Mommy and Daddy would talk to you and tell you about the world we wanted you to see.

There are so many things we love you for. We wish we

could have had a long life with you. But you're in heaven with all of the angels and saints. You play games and laugh all the time with all of your friends in heaven.

Mommy and Daddy know that you are happy in heaven, and we're learning to be happy here without you. We know that you are our angel and that you watch over Mommy and Daddy and baby brother OR sister all of the time.

Sophia, we wish you were here with us. We wish we could call your name and do all of the things we hoped for. But even though we can't, make sure you know that we love our little Baby Sophia forever and ever and ever.

Hugs and Kisses, baby. We love you.

Appendix C

My speech for Martha Weiss's GAPS at St. Kilian's in Farmingdale

Good evening everyone. Thank you for having me tonight. And thank you, Martha, for inviting me and asking me to share.

I have three daughters. Some dads complain about having all girls but I gotta say I don't know what they're talking about. I LOVE having all daughters. I wouldn't have it any other way.

I wouldn't have it any other way. Sometimes I have to force myself to believe this, but it's true.

Because, you see, Judith is our baby girl. She just turned 3. Charlotte is soon to be 8 — just saying that makes my knees buckle. And Sophia Michelle is the oldest sister. She was born on December 5 2008 — But — she was born still. After seven months in mama's belly, she was delivered — never to see the light of day. Never to see her mommy and her daddy smile at her. Never to feel the warmth of our hugging arms around her.

I have three daughters, but I feel guilty sometimes. I feel like I betray Sophia's memories when I typically tell people I have <u>two</u> daughters. Like — in my mind — I'm seeing the number THREE — while I'm saying the word two. I don't know why. Maybe it's not worth the awkwardness to tell people I have three children? Maybe I find it too emotional to say? Maybe it's just a "privacy" thing? I don't know.

But I HAVE three daughters.

My baby Sophia LIVED — you know. She lived for 28 weeks in the womb and thrilled Tara and me in countless ways. Sophia brought us joy and anxiety just like any child might — just like any child who learns to walk or talk, just like any child who bumps her head on the corner of the coffee table or falls from her bike or grows into a young woman and then gets her teenage heart broken by a boy.

Sophia lived. For a short but unforgettable time. She moved. I felt her. I saw her face. She grew! And She was picky too. She told Tara how to lay down at night. She told Tara that she didn't like marinara! Can you believe that? My wife — Tara CORRADO Flood couldn't eat marinara for 7 months! Sophia was a strong-willed baby. She heard our voices. We talked to her all the time. We sang to her a little Irish lullaby. We called her Little Birdy. She heard all of that and knew our voices. And I held her little body. And I kissed her forehead. And Tara and I dressed her and had her still life baptised. The priest at the hospital told me it wasn't necessary. She never took a breath. So her soul wouldn't be in peril. I said please. We said prayers and he anointed her. His name was Fr. Hyacinthe. He came from St. Mary of the Snows in Bellerose. I'll never forget him. Someday I want to find him and tell him what he means to me.

And after we lost Sophia, we visited her at St. Charles Cemetery every week for years, keeping her grave marker in so many of the ways that so many of us do. You know, it's interesting — there was a little community of parents in the Holy Innocents section of St. Charles. We met people there and talked about loss. We saw families grow. OUR family grew. We wondered where people went when we didn't see them at their markers for a while. We became friends with the ladies at Doreen's flowers on

Wellwood Avenue. The St. Charles Holy Innocents

neighborhood. I haven't been there in a while though.

But that's a life — isn't it? A pregnancy. A Joy, a delivery. A devastation. A funeral. Memories. That's a life.

Sophia lived.

But the past tense is what we all here struggle with. It's not the amount of time. I know we think it is sometimes, but it's not. It's like — if she had just gone full term, if I could have just held her warm body a single time, if I could have just had a few days....if we could have had just a little longer. Think of it this way — how much more time would have been enough with Sophia? Months? A year? 10 years? 25 years? 40 years? No. It's not enough. My parents, Tom and Kathie Flood, lost a child. Brian. My older brother. He was 24 years old. My parents' loss and Tara and my loss — though vastly different — are the same. The fact is that NO amount of time is enough when a child is concerned. It is said that outliving a child is the worst experience a parent can endure. And we have all tragically outlived our little babies.

No. It's not the amount of time. It's the past tense. That we have to admit that our child LIVED — that's what hurts.

I know how hard this is. And I don't always follow my own advice, but our language can determine our reality. We can make choices about how to perceive and report the events that unfold.

So, from the moment we noticed Tara was late. From the first visit to her ob and the first heart beat. From the first grainy sonogram. From the first little onesie we bought for our little angel we ARE parents. Not past tense. PRESENT tense.

I AM a parent.

You ARE a parent.

I HAVE three daughters.

These statements can define my reality. They're NOT lies. They are truths that are difficult to face, but I am NOT lying to myself when I say these things.

When I say these things to myself I feel empowered. I feel in control.

Of course, I know it's more complicated than I am admitting here. For example, if I say these things to others — to others who don't know our sadness and all our desperate attempts to cope or smile or go to work or keep from crying — or to GET OUT OF BED!! If I say these things in front of so many people who have no idea of the pain, the guilt, the shame, the emptiness of losing a child — honestly — I think there's a terror. I think that if I talk about my THREE daughters —about my first child who never saw the light of day — I think they feel a certain terror. They think, "oh my god, that can HAPPEN?" Some people truly might never hear of this happening to anyone. I don't pretend to think that they don't KNOW someone who has suffered this worst of all pains. I just think that they simply don't hear about it. No one's allowed to talk about it.

We have been made very aware of the popular aversion to hearing about the sadness of what most expect to be a joyous occasion. We have learned NOT to talk about our babies. Our pregnancies. The "high risk" doctors we hunted down. Mommy's hilarious cravings. Our nesting. The maternity clothes mommy bought. The baby clothes we bought. The furniture we ordered. ALL of the things we did because we ARE parents. HERE we can talk about all of those things. In this group. With each other. But not always out there. Not with so many people who are terrified by our pain.

The result — in my experience — has been a profound sense of loneliness. Loneliness. From friends. Colleagues. Acquaintances. From family. From neighbors and community. From spouses, life partners, soul mates. The loneliness we feel drives us away from even those people — that person — whom we need most to heal.

So if we can combat that loneliness, then we might achieve some much needed healing.

I will always cherish my experience with Tara in a bereavement group after Sophia. In that environment we were able to speak so candidly with the other members. We talked about fears and regrets. We talked about profound sorrow. We talked about guilt and embarrassment.

You know what I remember? No one in that group tried to make anyone “feel better”. We accepted each other’s grief. We listened to each other’s pain. Laughed at jokes. I didn’t feel lonely at those meetings. I felt like I was amongst friends.

And though our lives have, understandably, moved away from each other, I believe there’s always that bond. What groups like these and events like this, like tonight, remind us is that while the loneliness we feel is overwhelming — and real — we, at times, can be comforted that we are not alone. While we would never choose someone else’s pain to be a source of our comfort — in our cases, it is. Our losses are each other’s comfort. My daughter’s name is Sophia. What’s your child’s name? Here with each other — combat loneliness — we’re not alone. Our babies, our angels, are friends! We have dropped OUR babies off at heaven for an eternal playdate. We are their parents. We ARE their parents. Not past tense.

I hope I’m not being too pushy. But I don’t imagine that I’m the only one here who feels an instant bond with someone who has lost a baby. It’s not always socially acceptable to do so but when I learn of someone’s loss — sometimes I just want to give a hug and say — Me too.

Me too.

Shortly after Tara and I lost Sophia, a student of mine — an 11th grader — came up to me after class and gave me an envelope. She said — it’s from my mom. She said her mom worked with parents who’d lost their babies. The contents of the envelope were some materials she had regularly shared.

She hoped they'd help. That girl's name was Chrissy. Chrissy Weiss. Her mother — of course — is Martha Weiss, who has helped so many of us with our losses. But I hadn't met Martha by then.

Some time later — it might have been a few years — I was walking through the lobby of my school when I saw a woman signing—in at the desk. I overheard her say her last name — Weiss — so I stopped and asked if she were Chrissy's mother. When she said yes, I introduced myself. What do you think she did? Of course, she gave me a hug. In the middle of the hallway. She gave me a hug. And I knew while she hugged me she was thinking — Me too.

Me too

I AM a parent

I am NOT alone.

Our language can establish our reality. I believe this. Yes — The loss of a child can distort and confuse reality. That distortion is a result of our broken hearts. Our broken minds. But I think we can change our hearts by changing the language we use and the contexts in which we speak about our angels.

So...

Me too.

I AM a parent.

I am NOT alone.

I HAVE three daughters.

Sophia lived.

Sophia LIVED? No Sophia LIVES. Not the way we had wished. But she LIVES: In my heart. In Tara's heart. In the hearts of Sophia's grandparents. In a remembrance like tonight. In an awareness walk. In every candle lit for her. In a brick we laid for her. In a tattoo. In a bracelet or a charm necklace. In a grave marker.

She lives.

Tara and I host a toy drive every December in Sophia's

name. The Sophia Michelle toy drive. We donate toys to the Toys For Tots foundation. It's just a little thing. It's open to anyone but it's mostly friends and family and neighbors: some people that know about our loss and others who learn about it. But we do it each year, and it keeps Sophia's memory alive. I'm giving this speech right now to keep my baby's name alive. Sophia Michelle. Now — Sophia — LIVES in every one of your minds. I have introduced her to you. Put her name in your memory and let her live there. Share your child's name with someone. Share your child's name with me. Say it now. Aloud. Tell your story. Tell your angel's story. Let your story, your language, the words you use determine your reality. And I will too.

We all here have experienced a TRAUMATIZING event. I held my lifeless daughter. I put my face to her cold still skin. Tara and I had everything we hoped for, believed in, trusted — shaken. Disrupted. Suspended. But here we are, now the parents of Sophia's two little sisters. While we were terrified about "trying again" — and we wondered if we could ever dare to — something compelled us. No matter how hurt we were, in spite of our inexplicable loss and sadness, something compelled us to try again. To love. To trust. To believe. To restore our faith in all that seemed to have forsaken us.

I don't have to accept the sadness I feel. I don't have to accept the loneliness I feel. Yes, I have to accept that my little girl Sophia died. And I have to accept that every day. And I experience all of the accompanying emotions. But the life I live doesn't have to be governed by loss.

I have three daughters.

I wouldn't have it any other way.

I am not alone.

My daughter Sophia Michelle lives — in my heart.

About a year ago I spoke for a similar remembrance at North Shore LIJ. To close my thoughts tonight, I want to share just a small part of that talk with you:

I just want you all to know that I consider you my friends now. We're in a fraternity of suffering — Or maybe it's a fraternity of healing. In either case, you're friends of mine now. And your angels and my angel are now up in heaven giggling and playing together. I don't know if you believe in heaven. It doesn't matter. I know Sophia's in a place. I know it. It's a place where the carpet is made of clouds and stars float in front of the children's faces like lightning bugs and the sun says good morning and the crescent moon wears a nightcap — If your loss is recent, I know my daughter, and she is up there right now welcoming your little baby. And if your loss is old, Sophia is jumping rope or blowing bubbles with a giant bubble wand. That's what she does now. I know it.

Thank you everyone for helping me heal tonight.

About the Author

M.J. Flood is a husband and a father of two little girls and a baby angel. Residing in Long Island, New York, he is a high school literature and writing teacher and the author of *Where Are You? Finding Myself in My Greatest Loss*, his first published work.

Flood is also the writer/director of *Too Much Noise* — a short film in American Sign Language — which has appeared in several film festivals and won the Best Original Idea award at New York City's 2018 Chain Film Festival.

M. J. Flood, "A Father's Voyage to the Moon – Without His Baby Girl," *Still Standing Magazine* (March 11, 2019)

Made in the USA
Middletown, DE
06 November 2019

78070881R00097